Coloring Books for Grownups

Día De Los Muertos

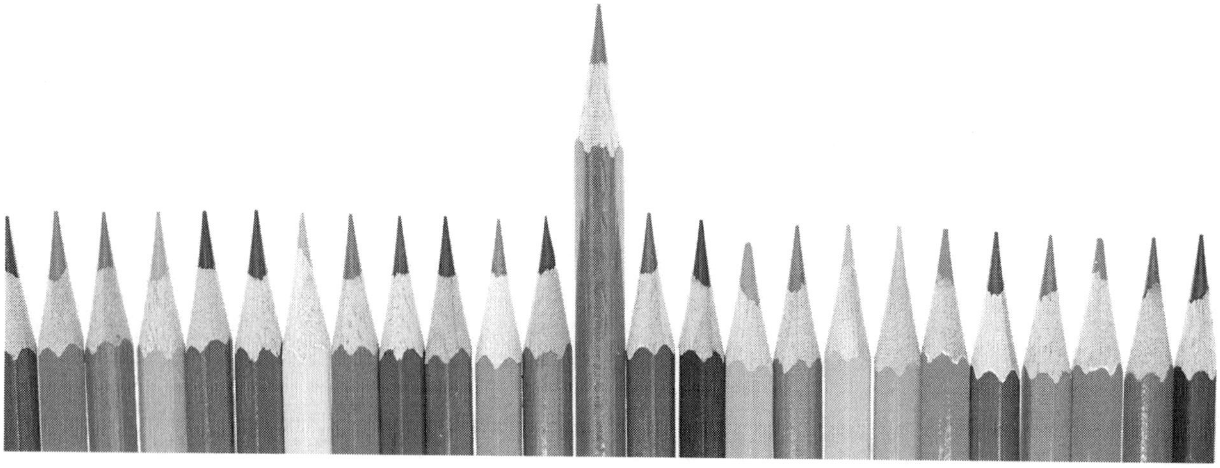

Chiquita publishing

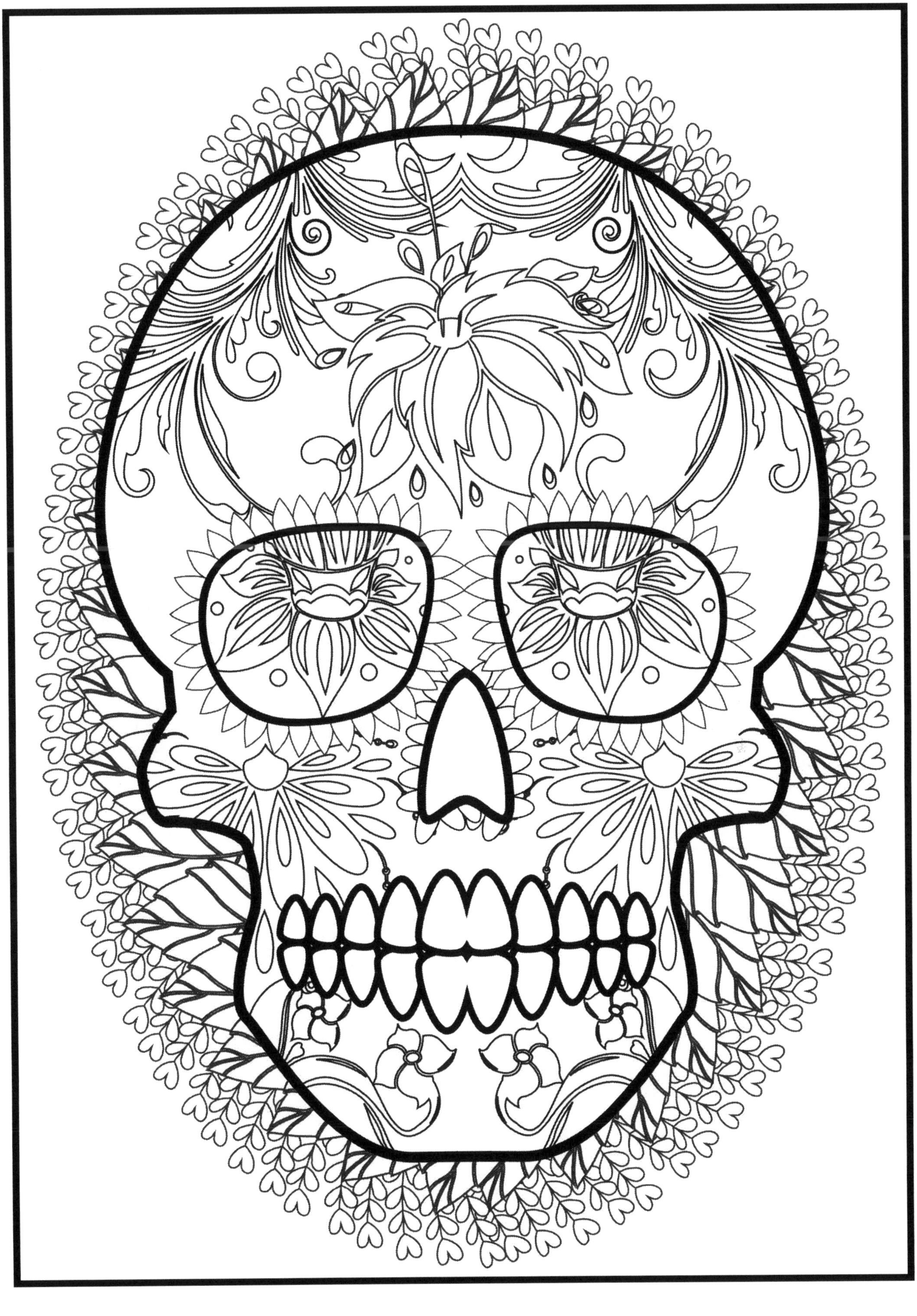

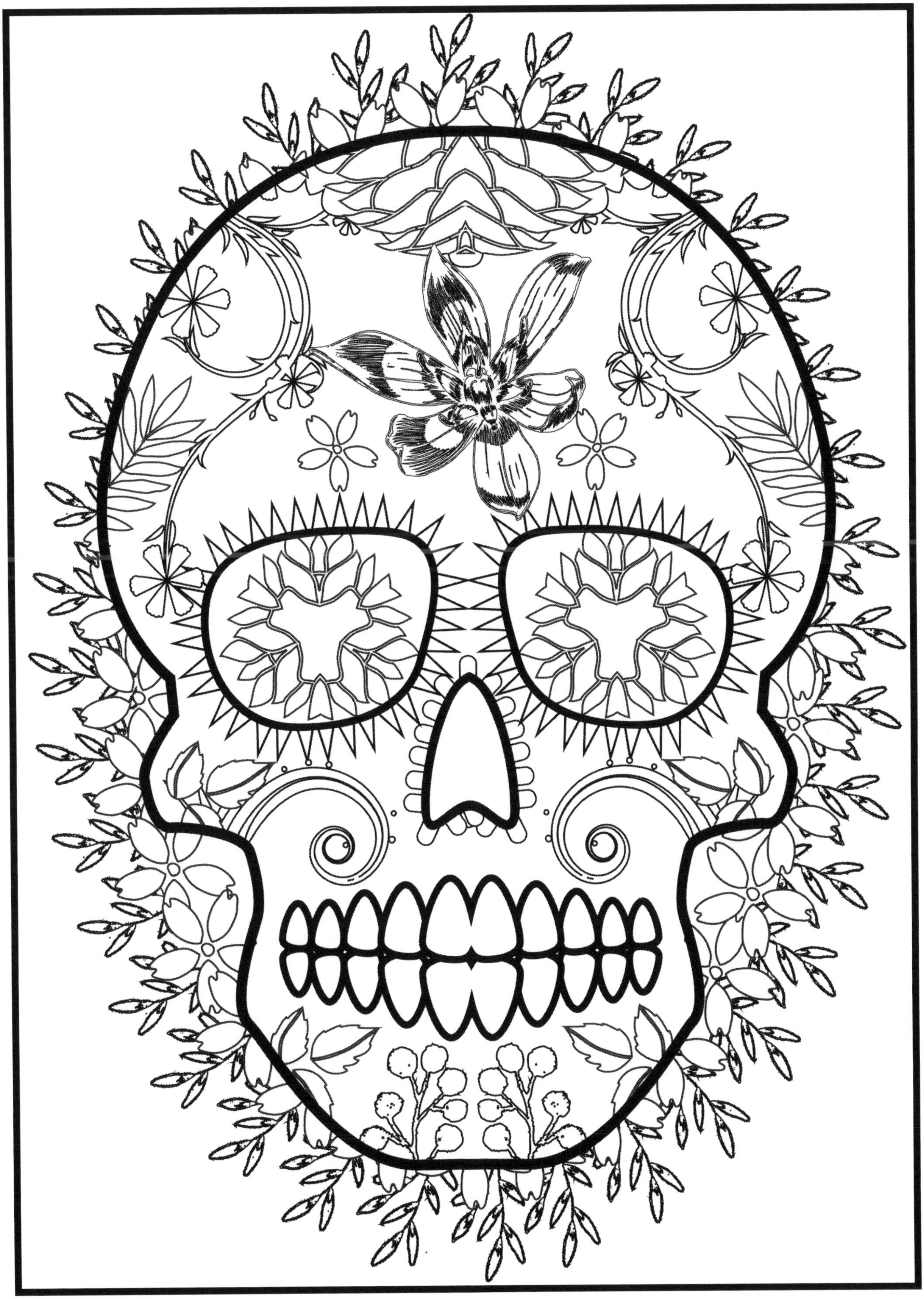

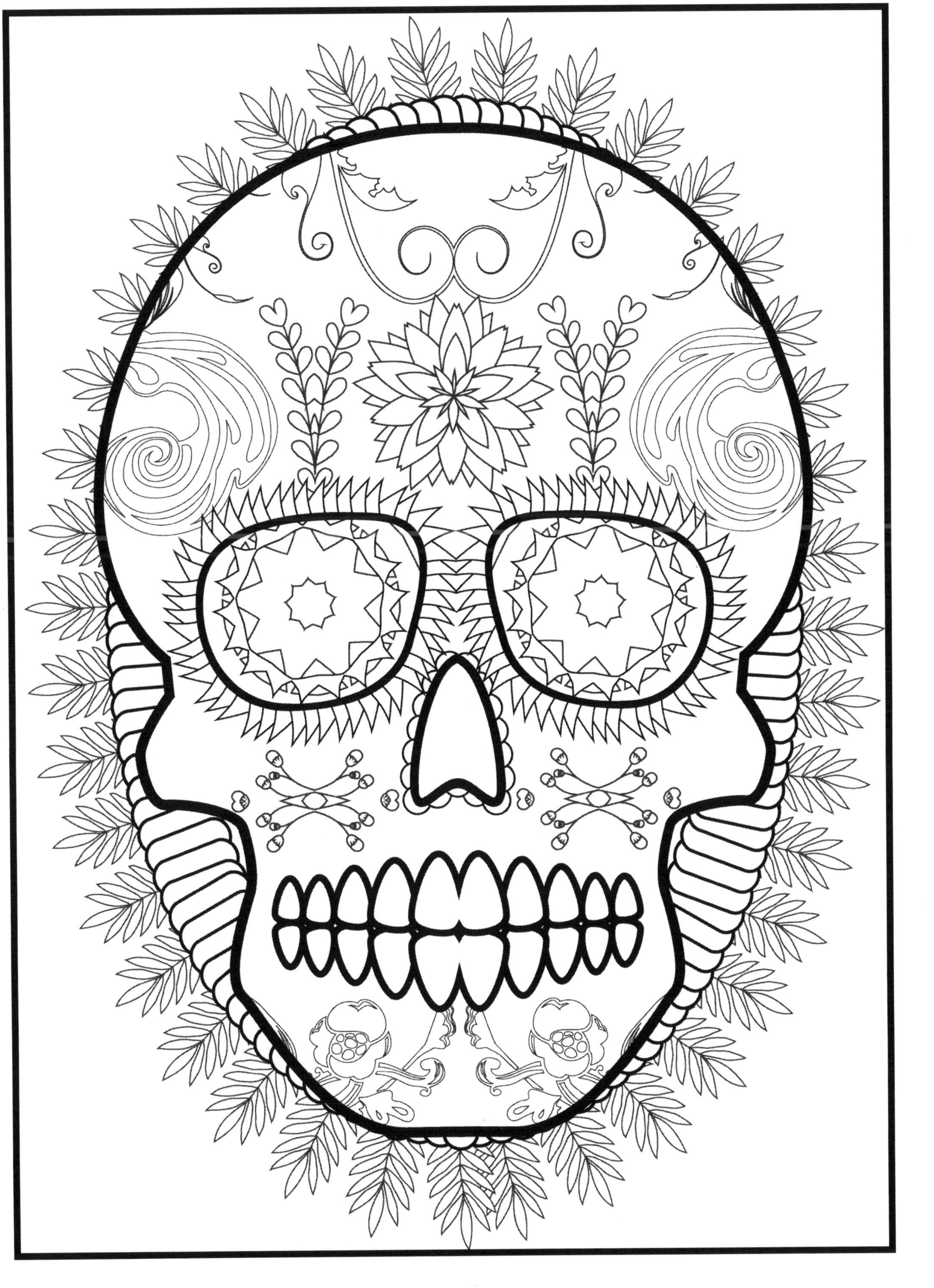

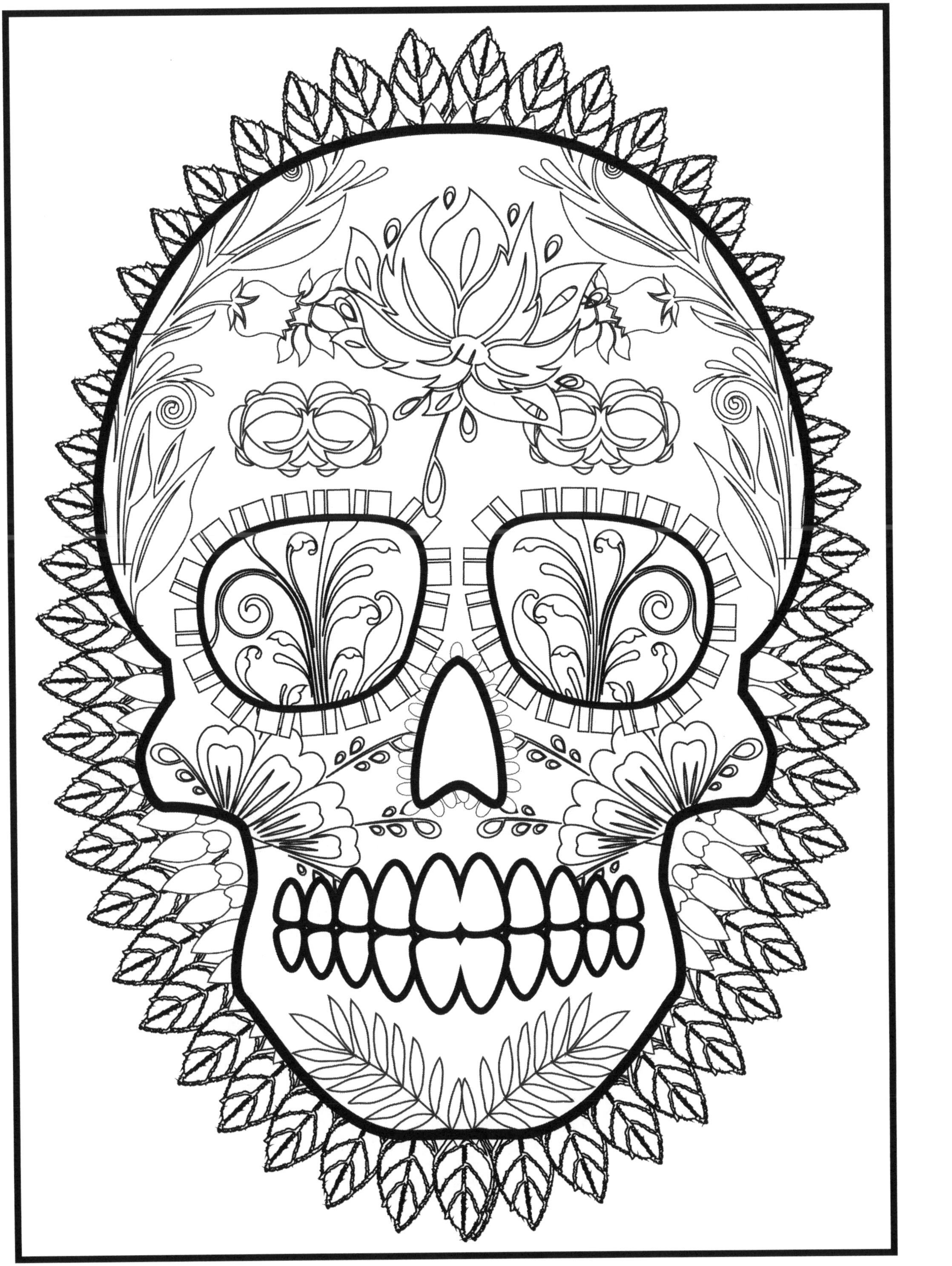

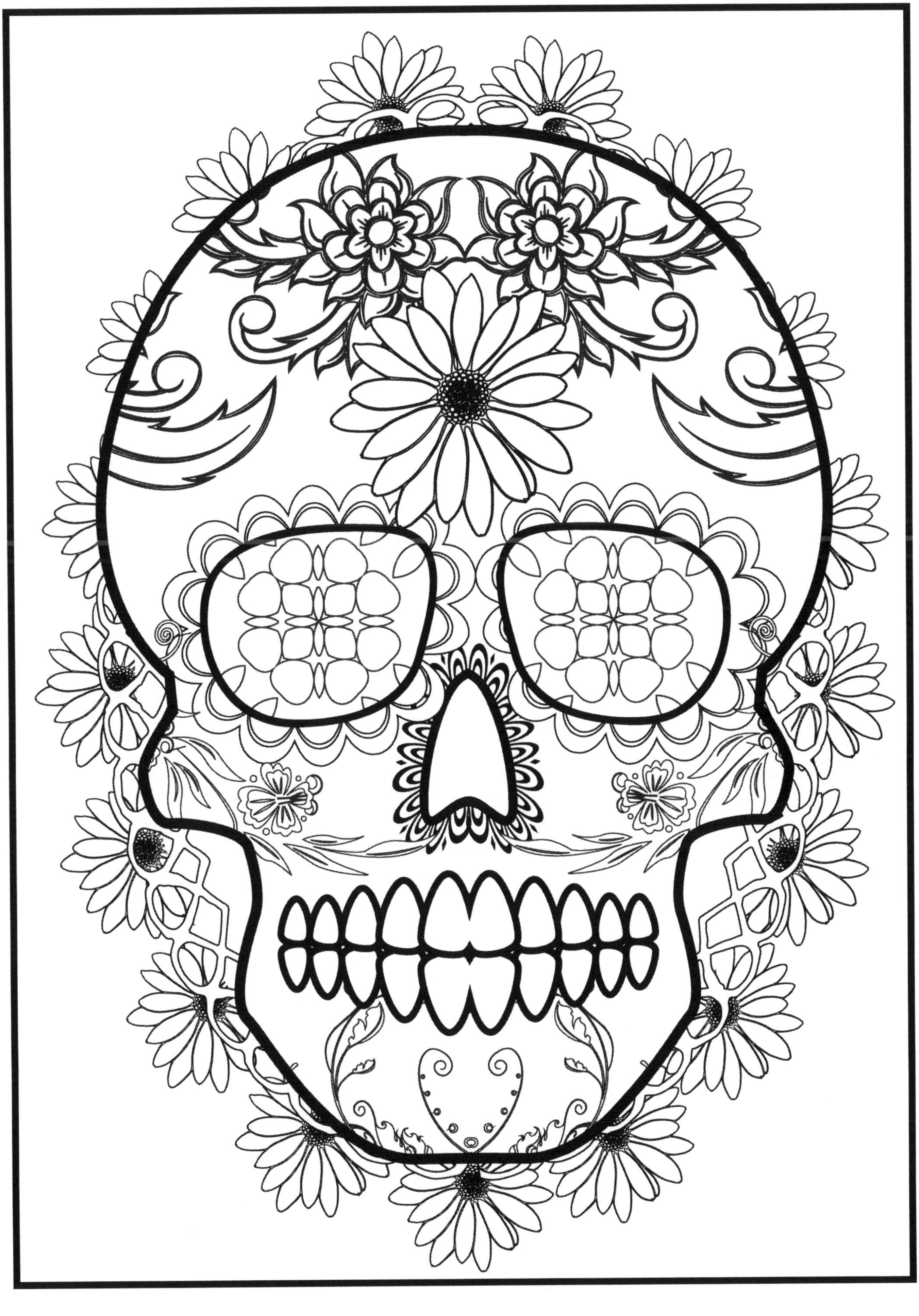

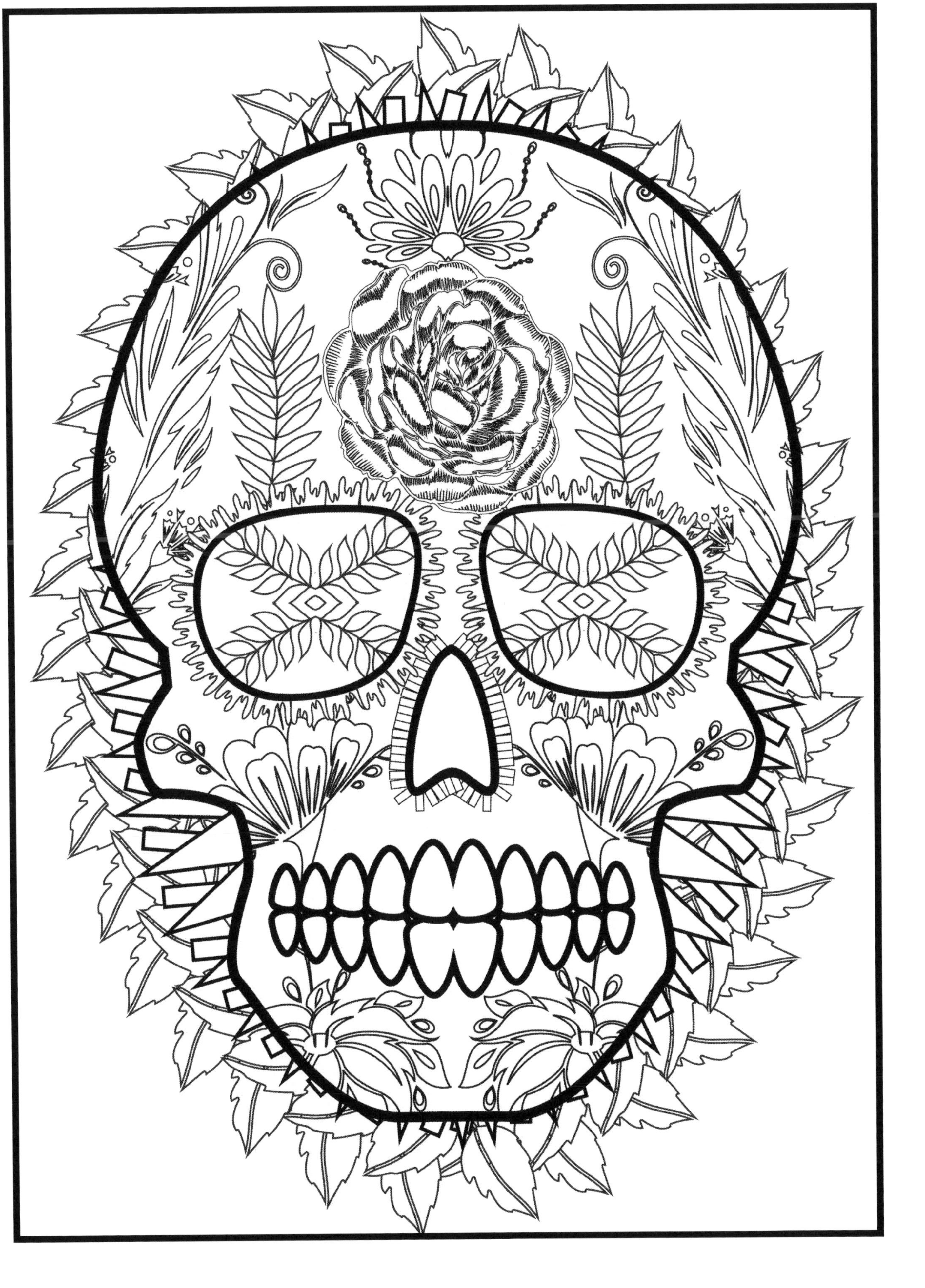

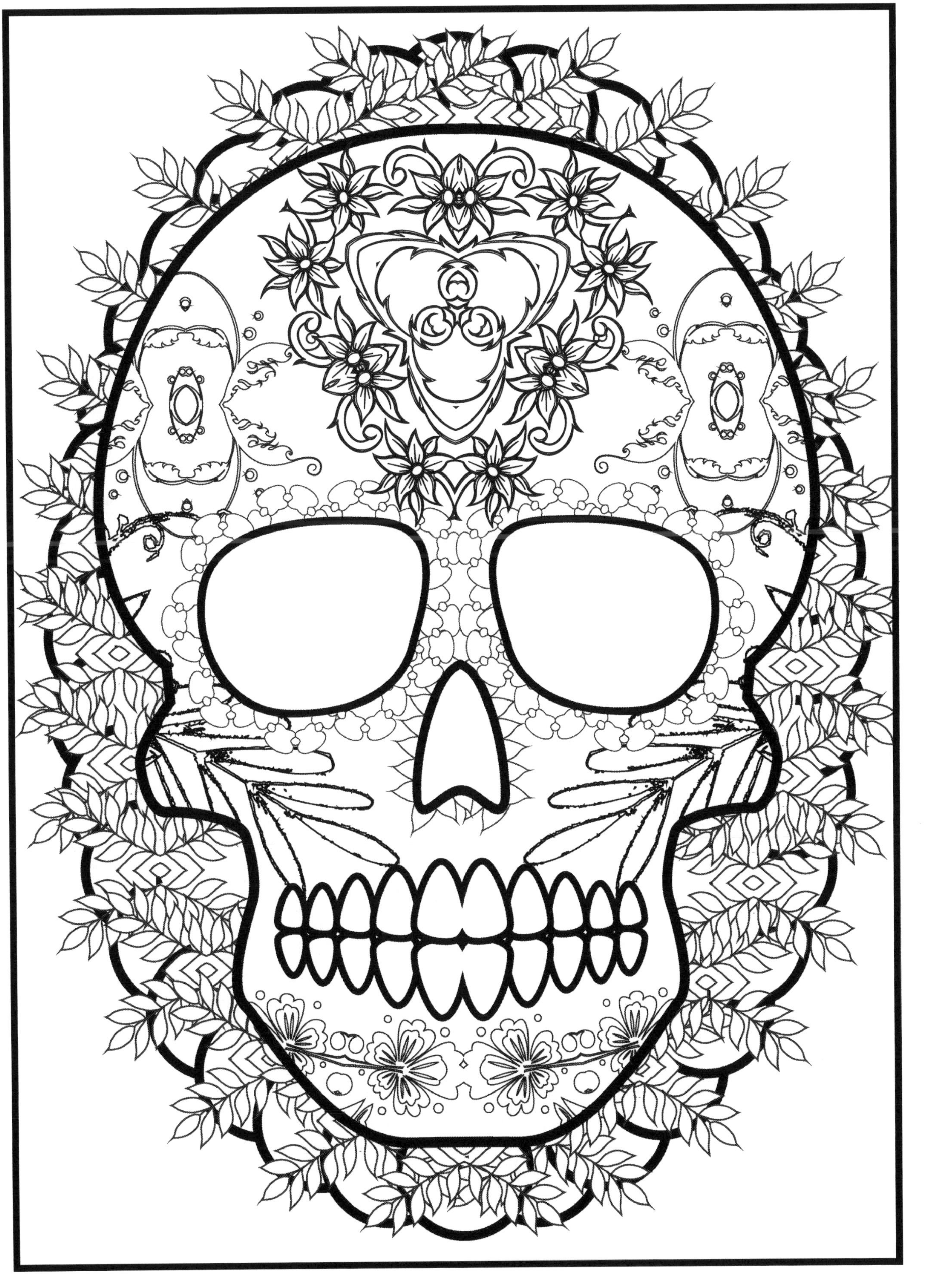

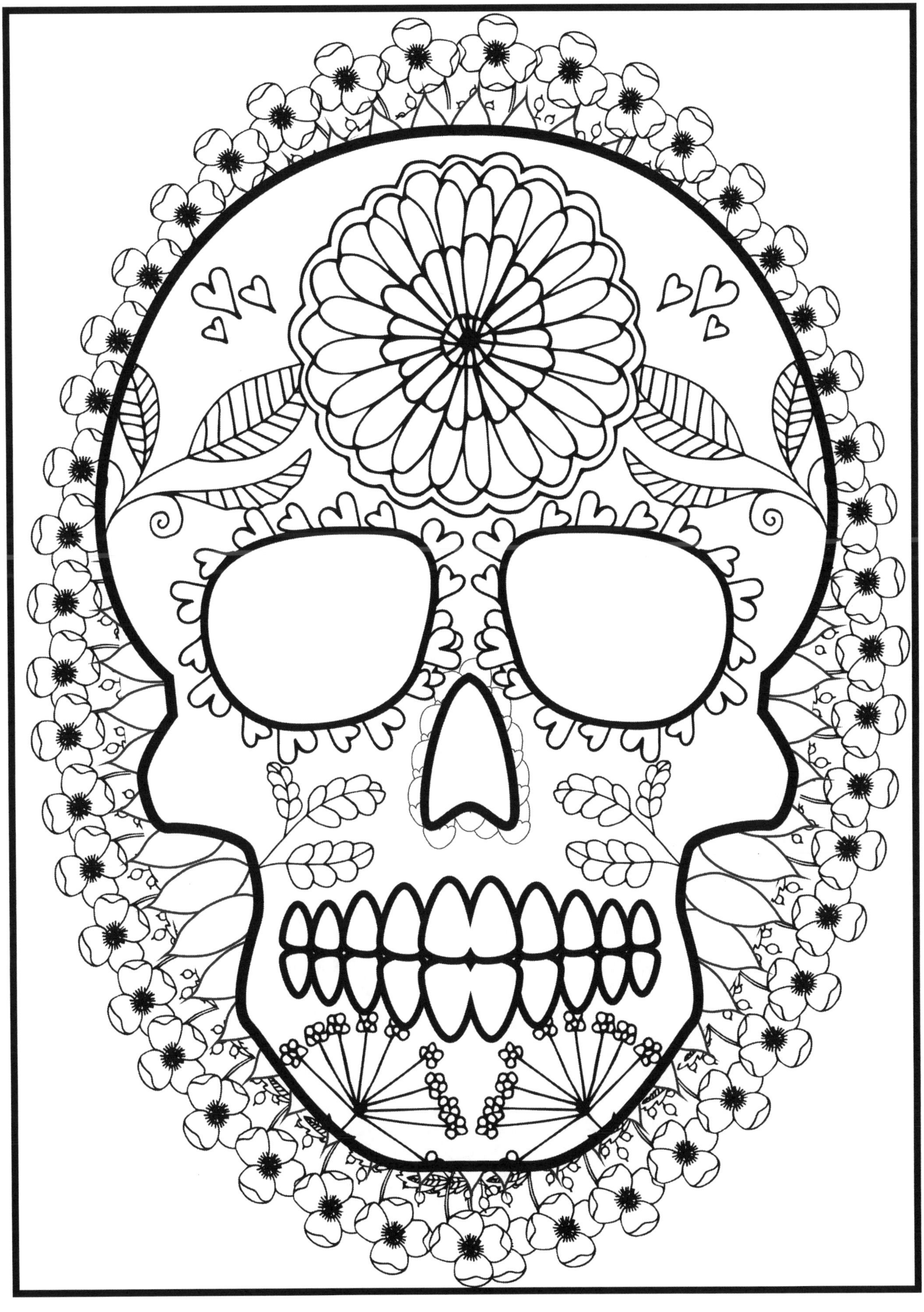

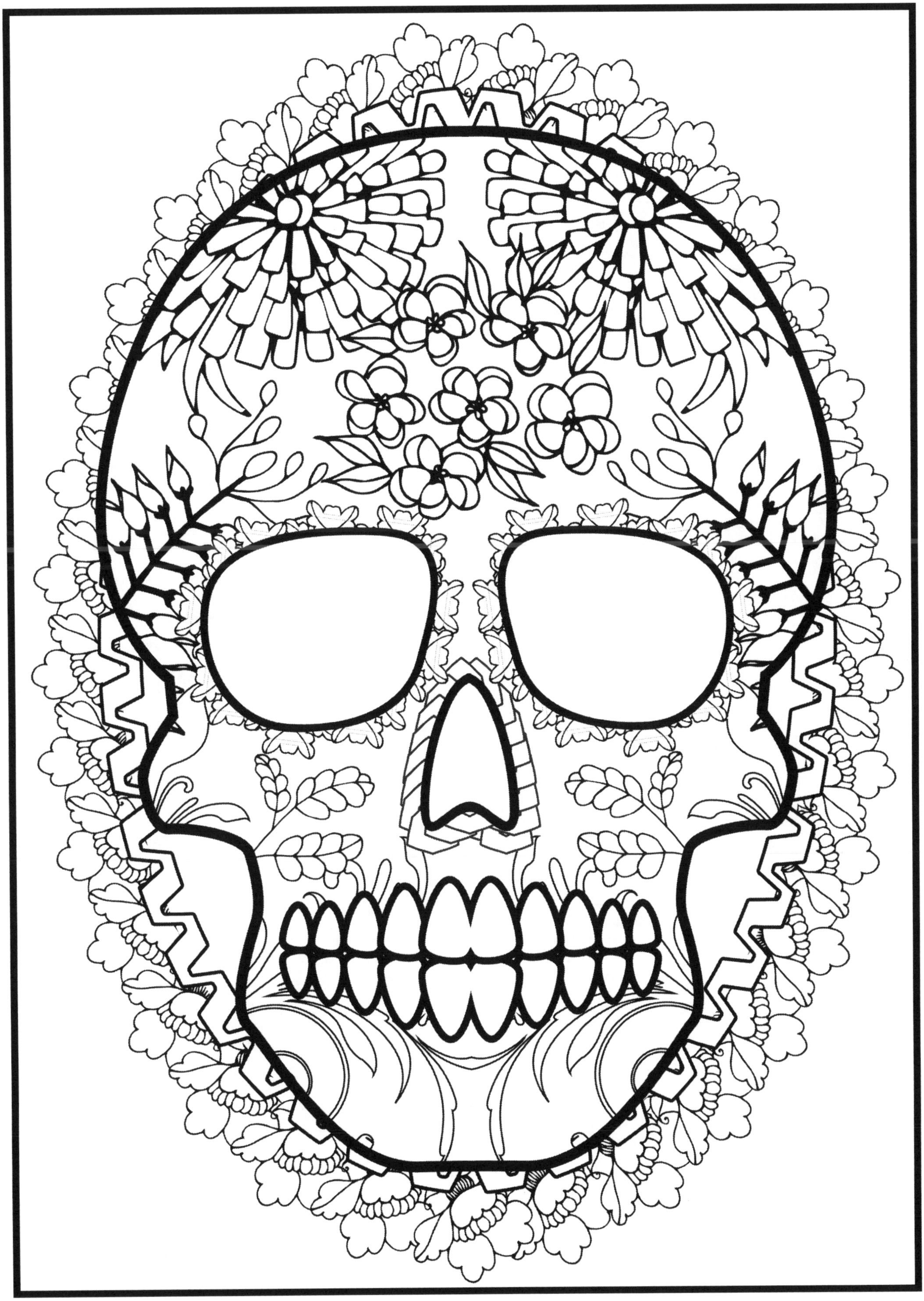

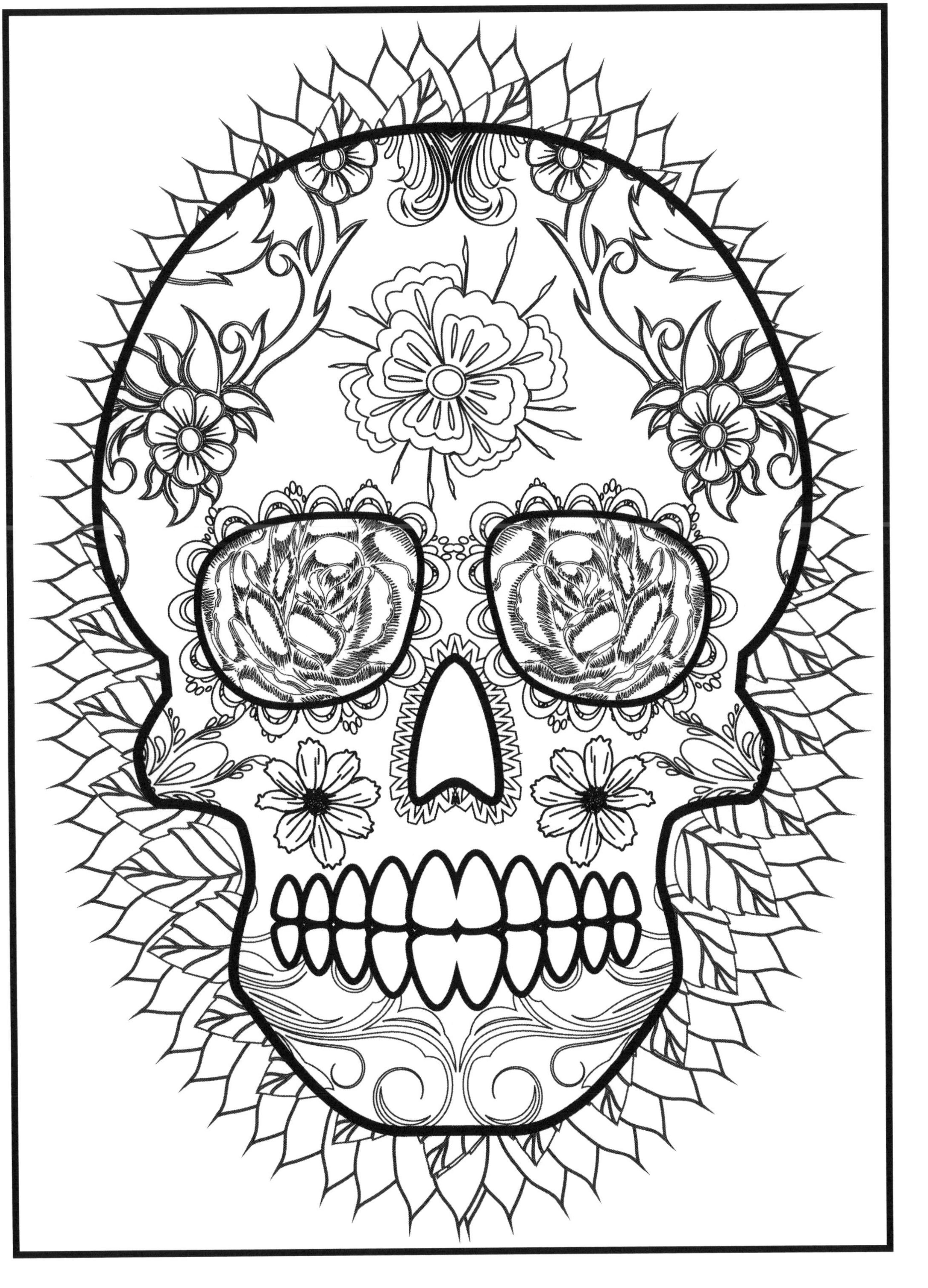

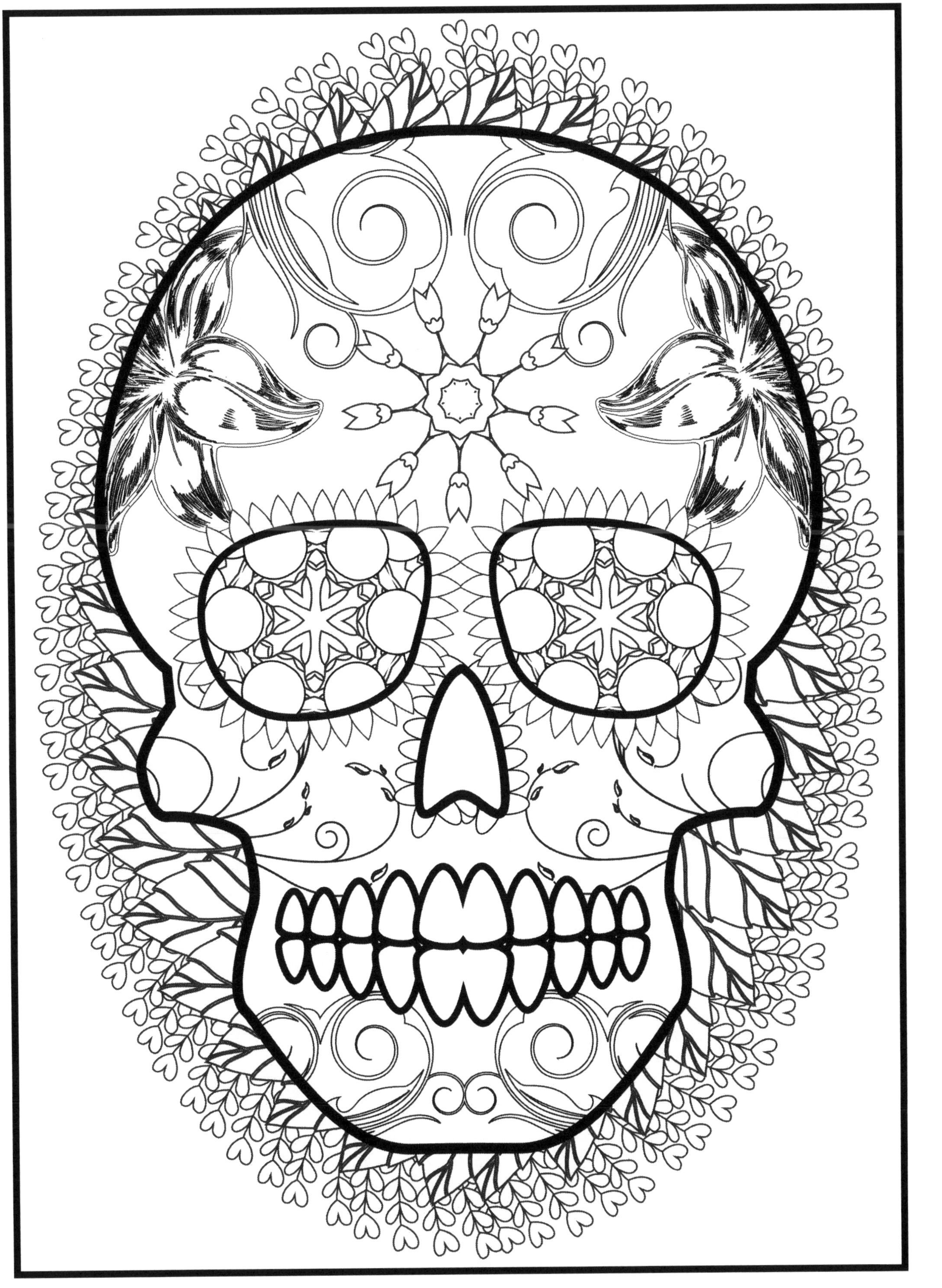

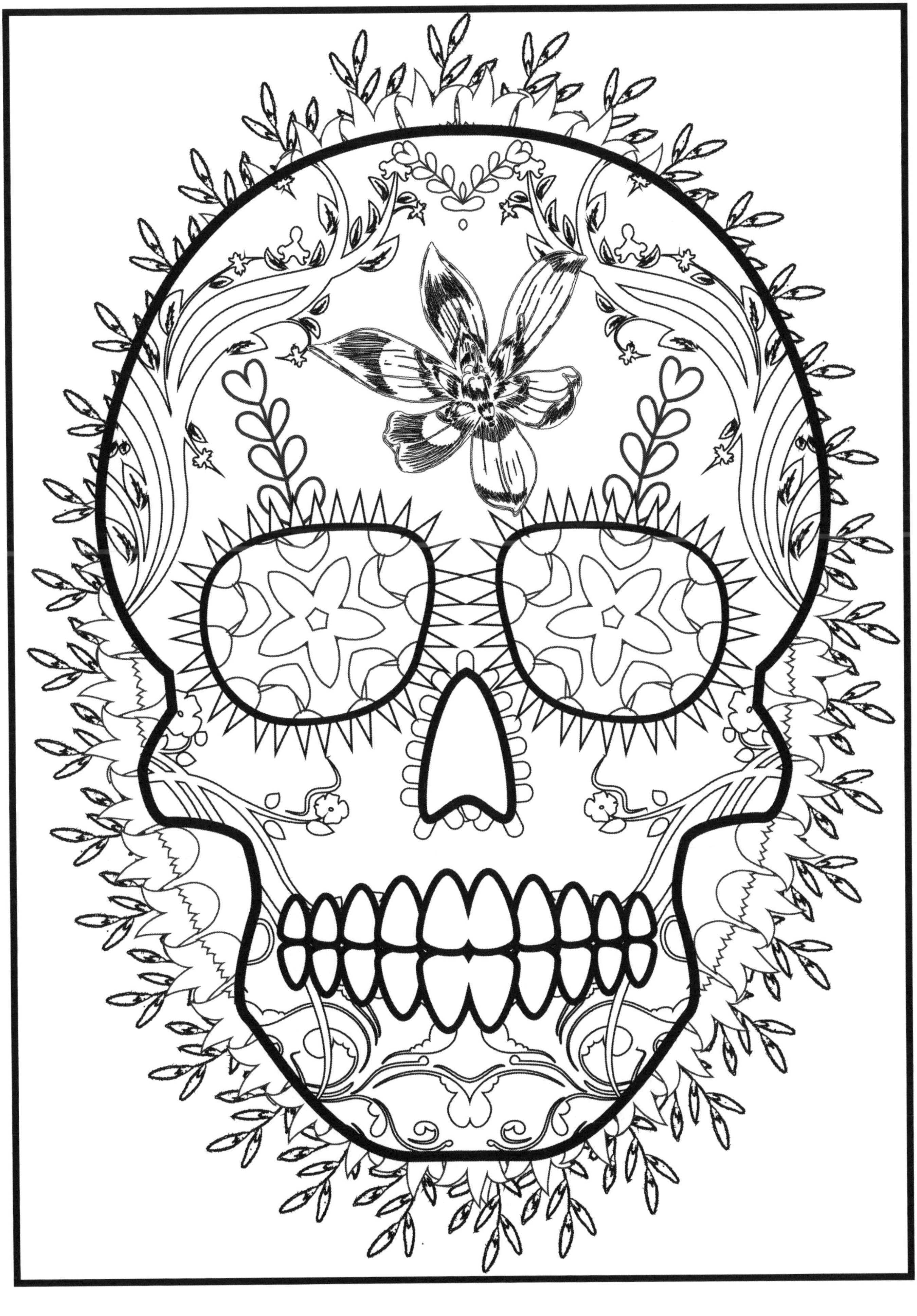

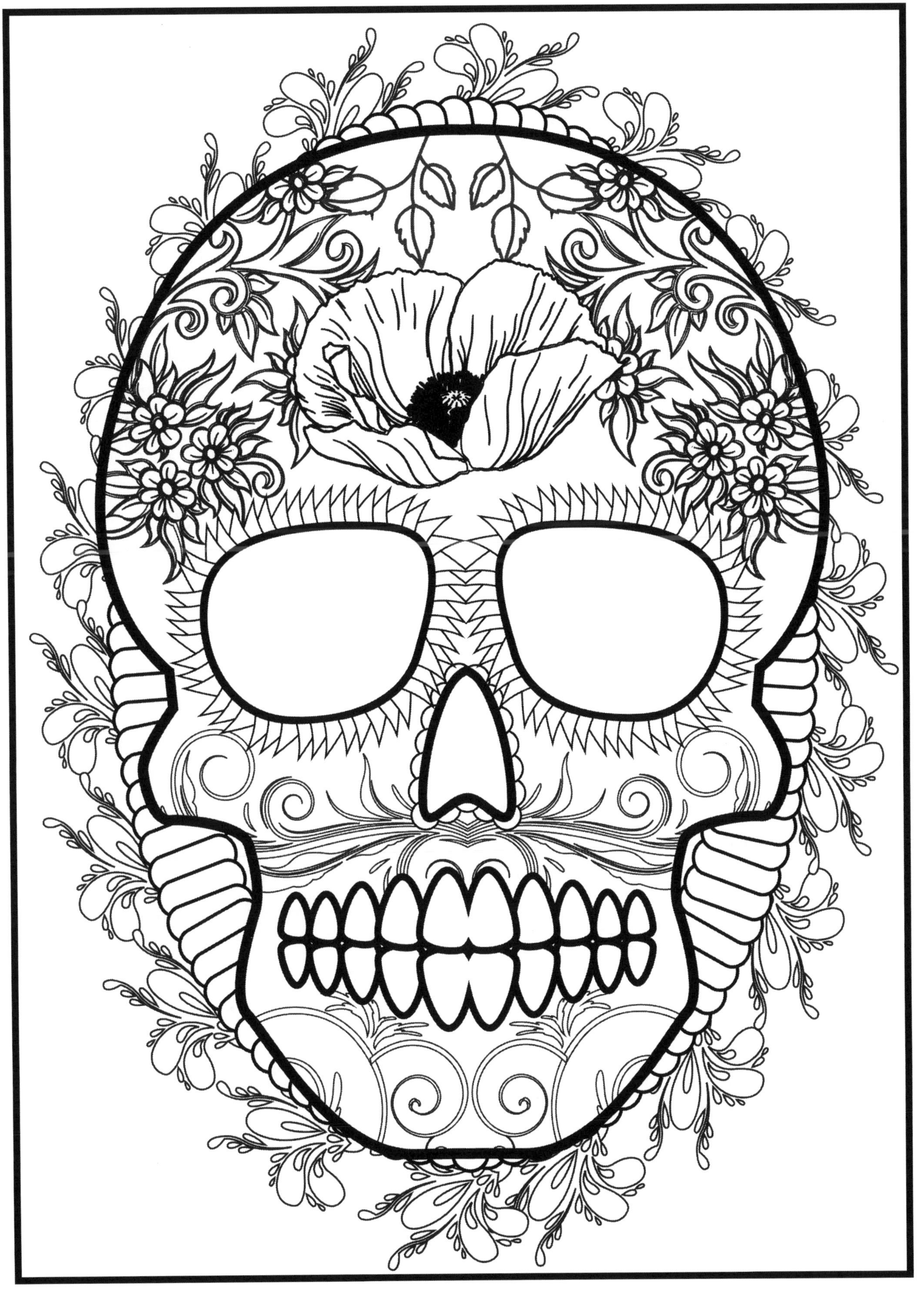

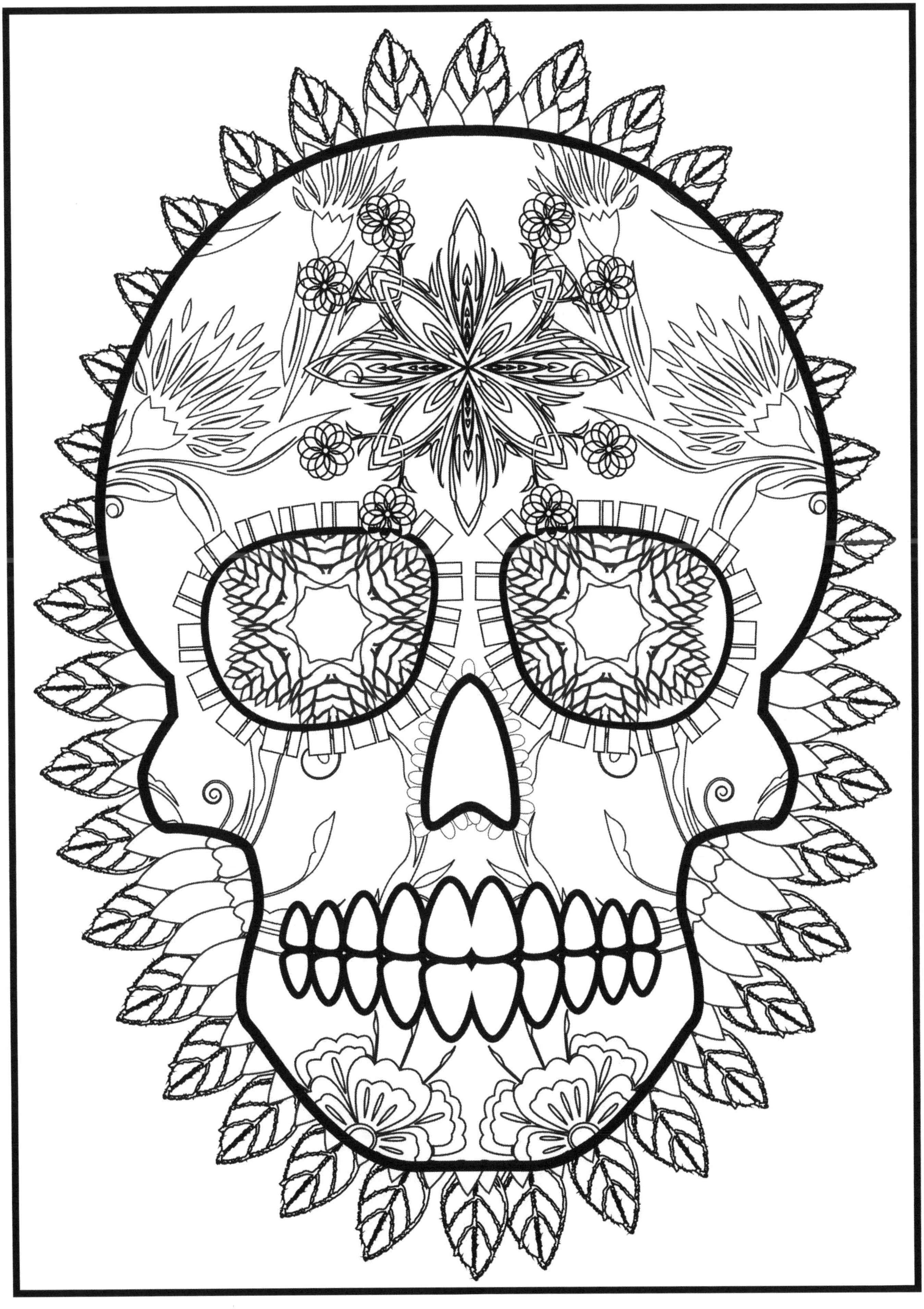

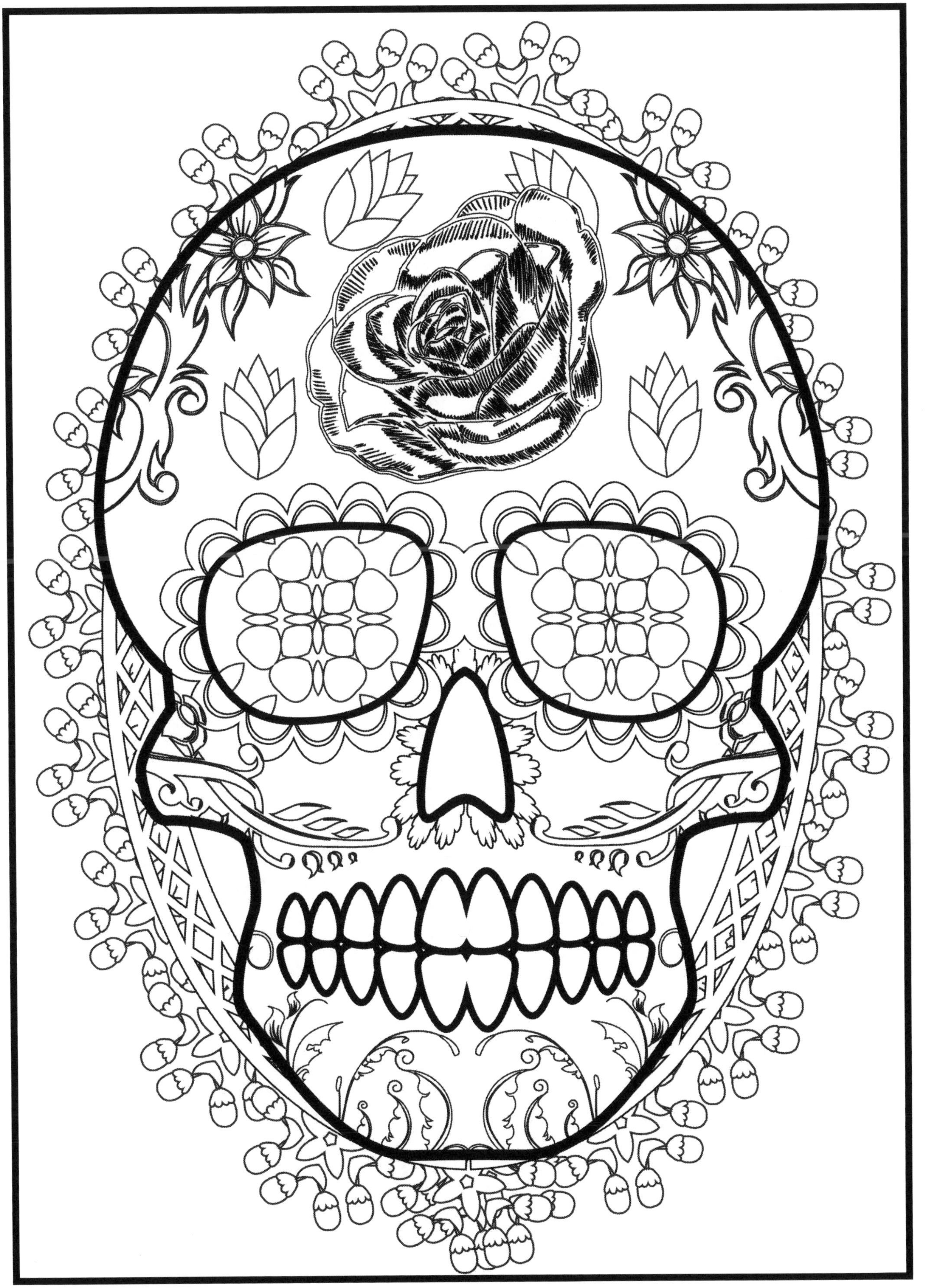

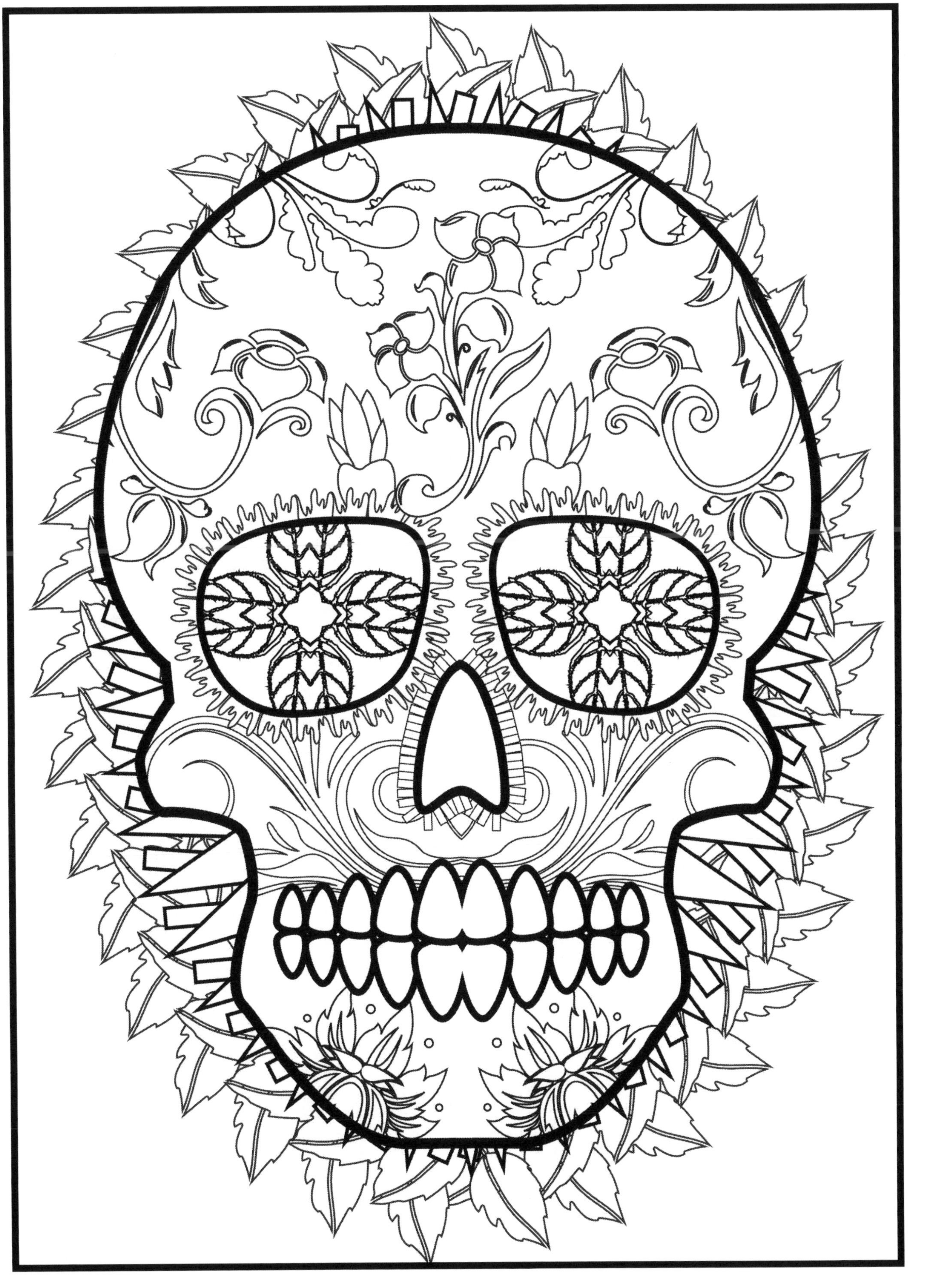

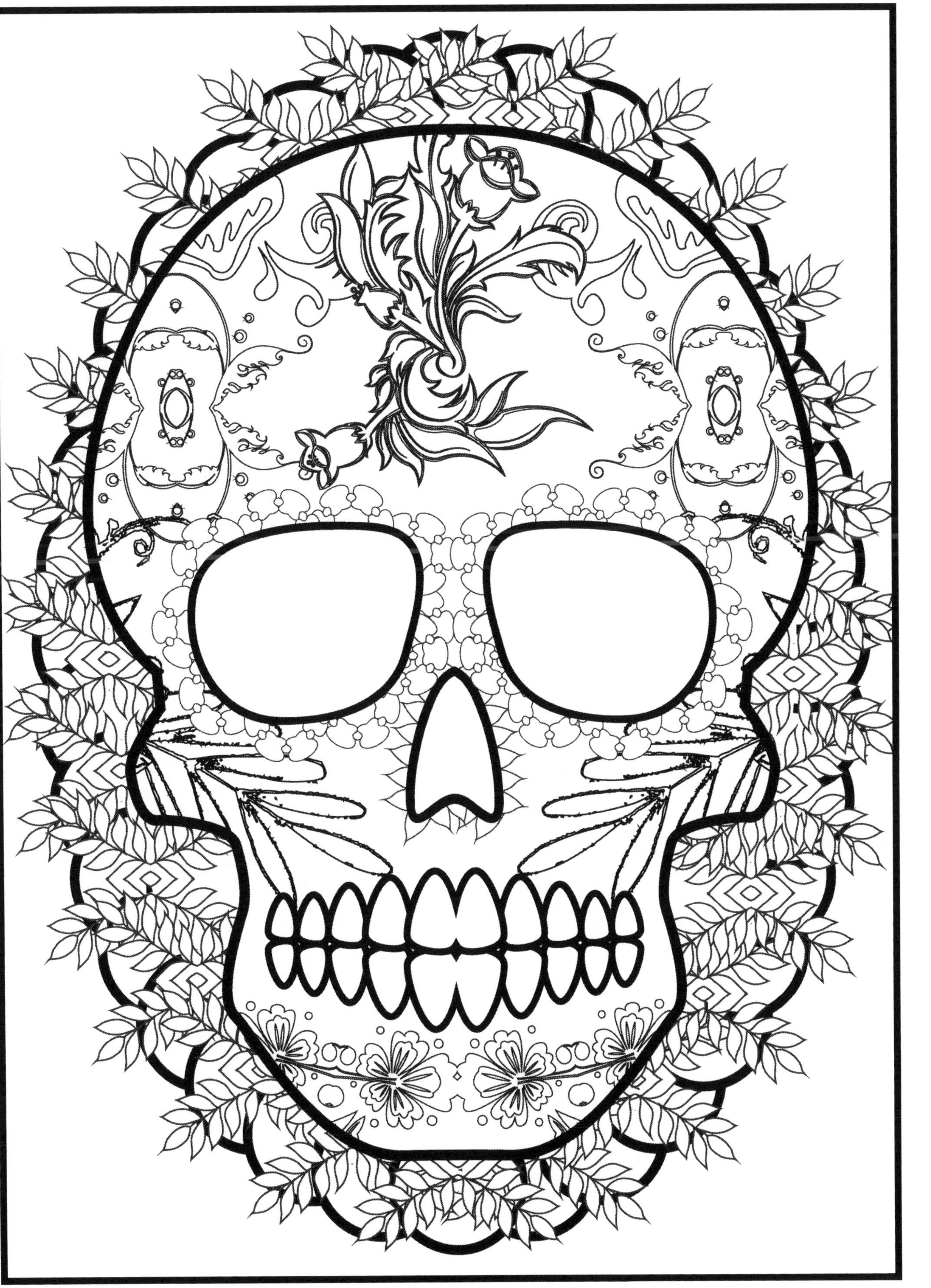

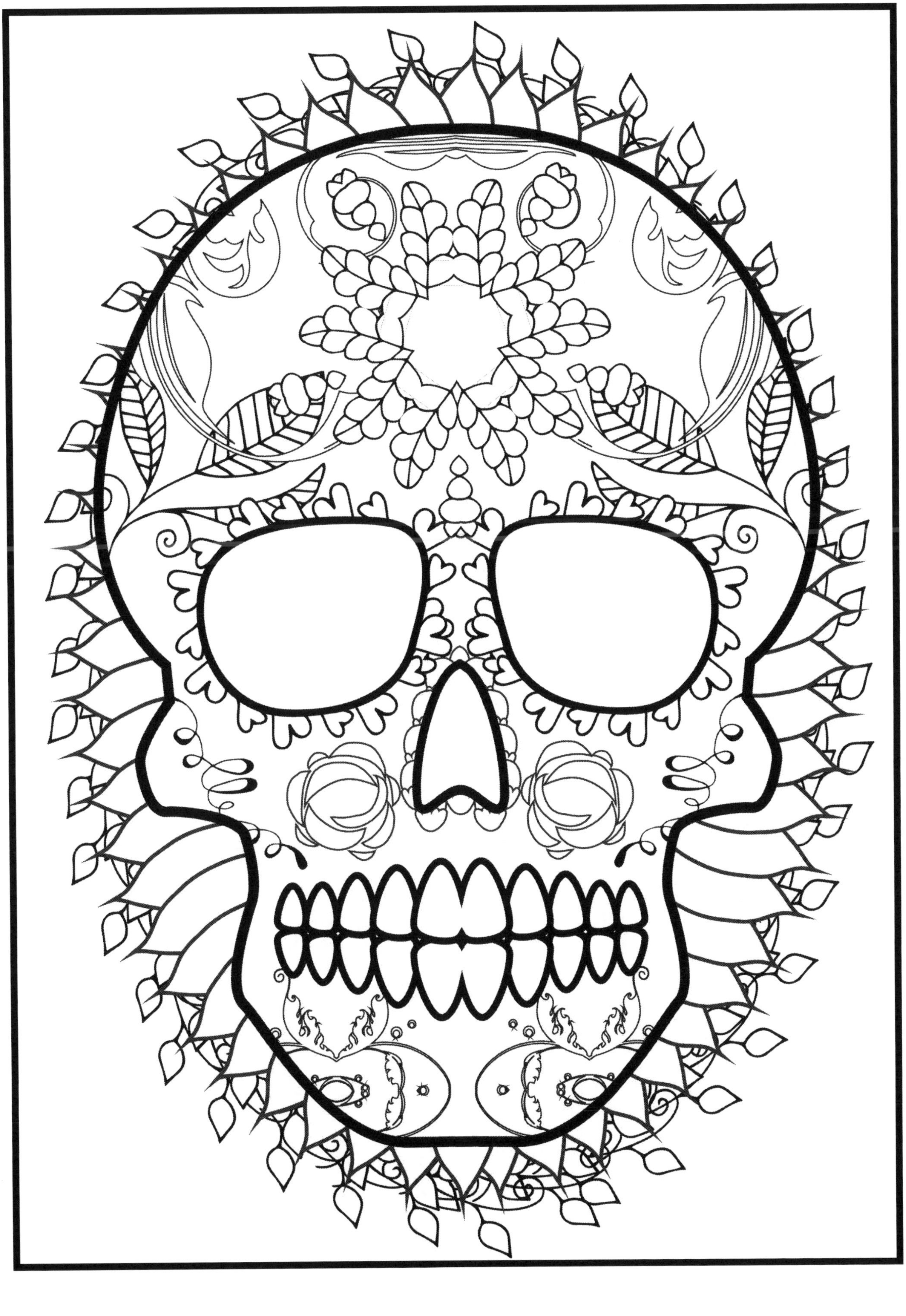

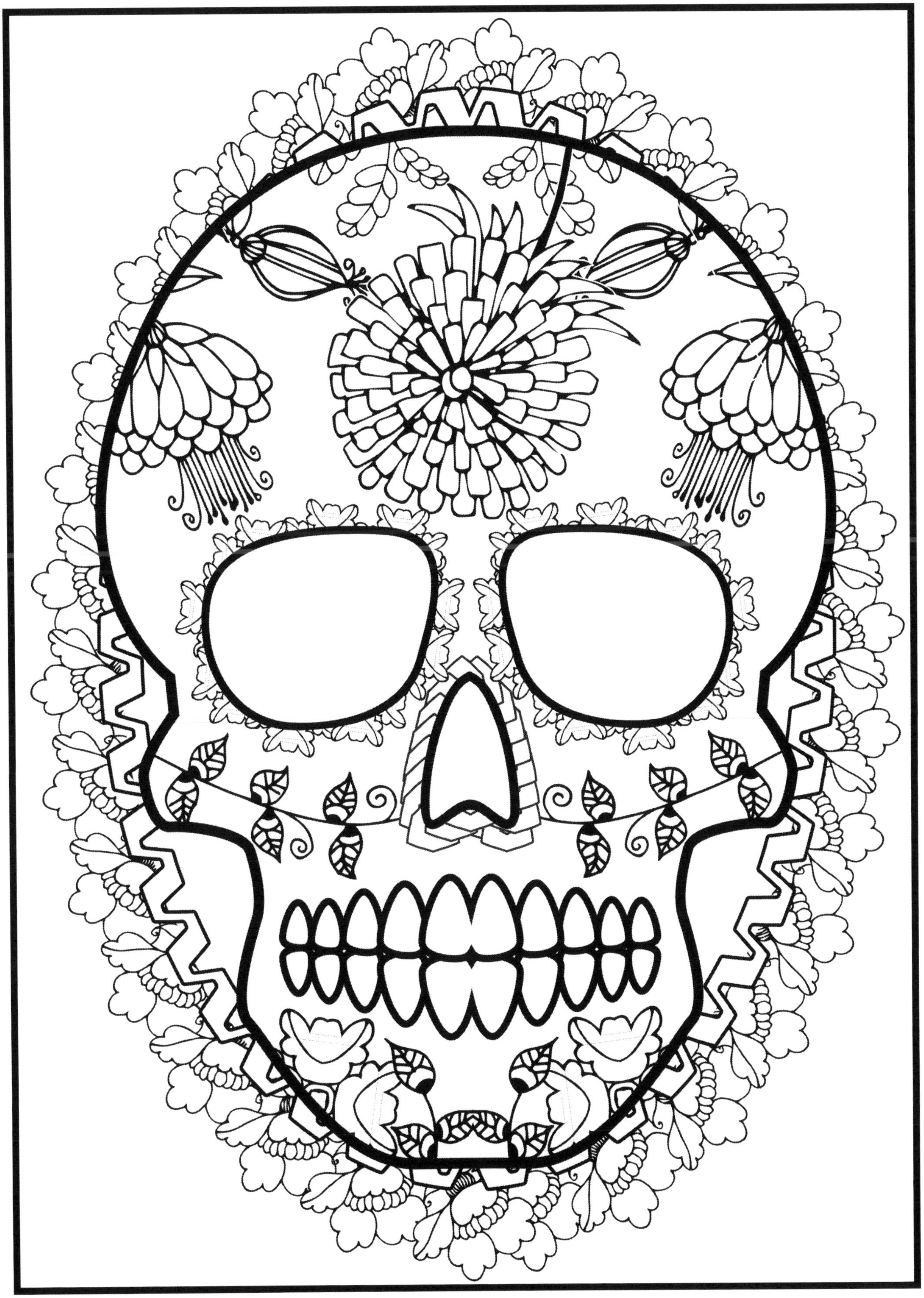

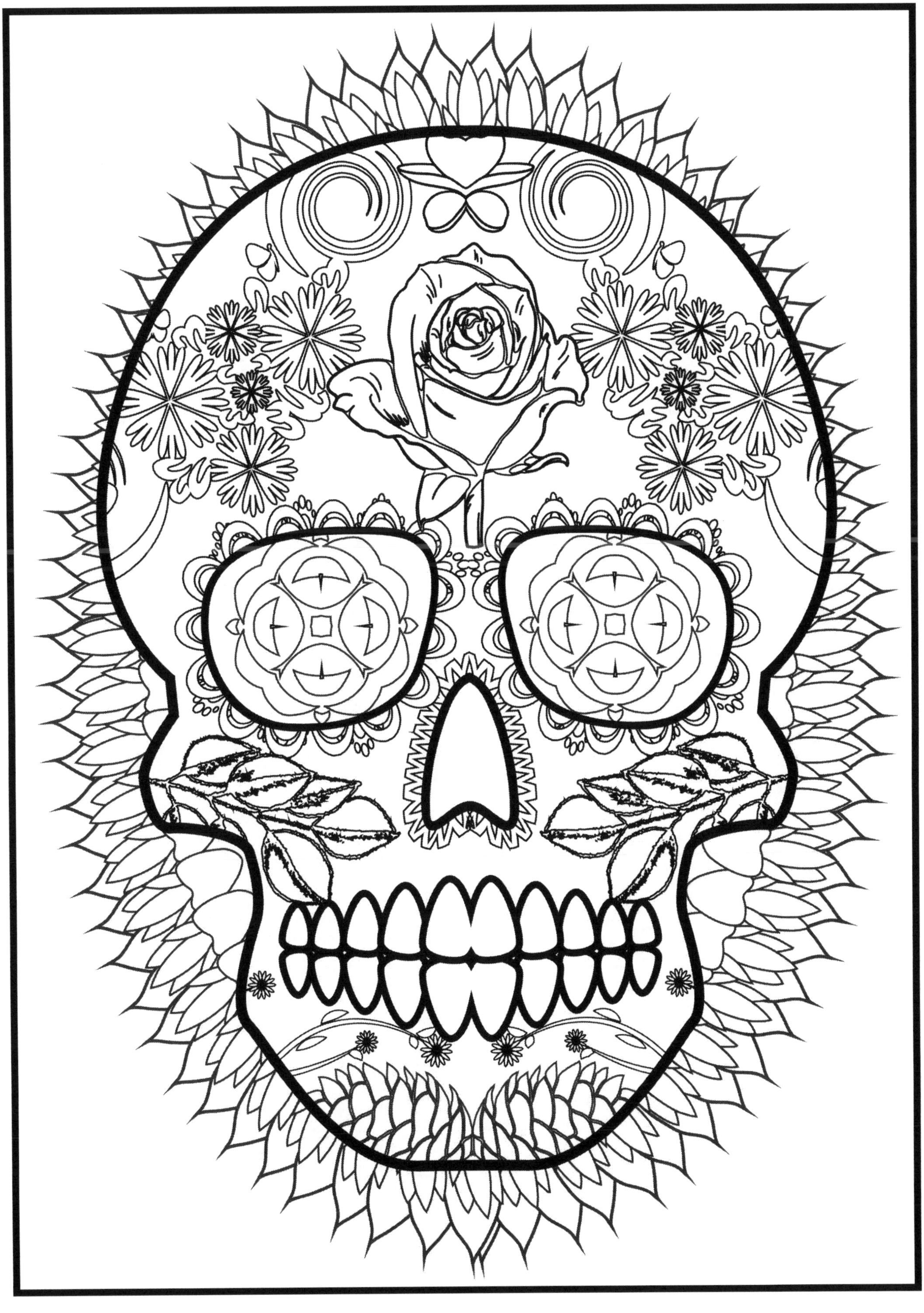

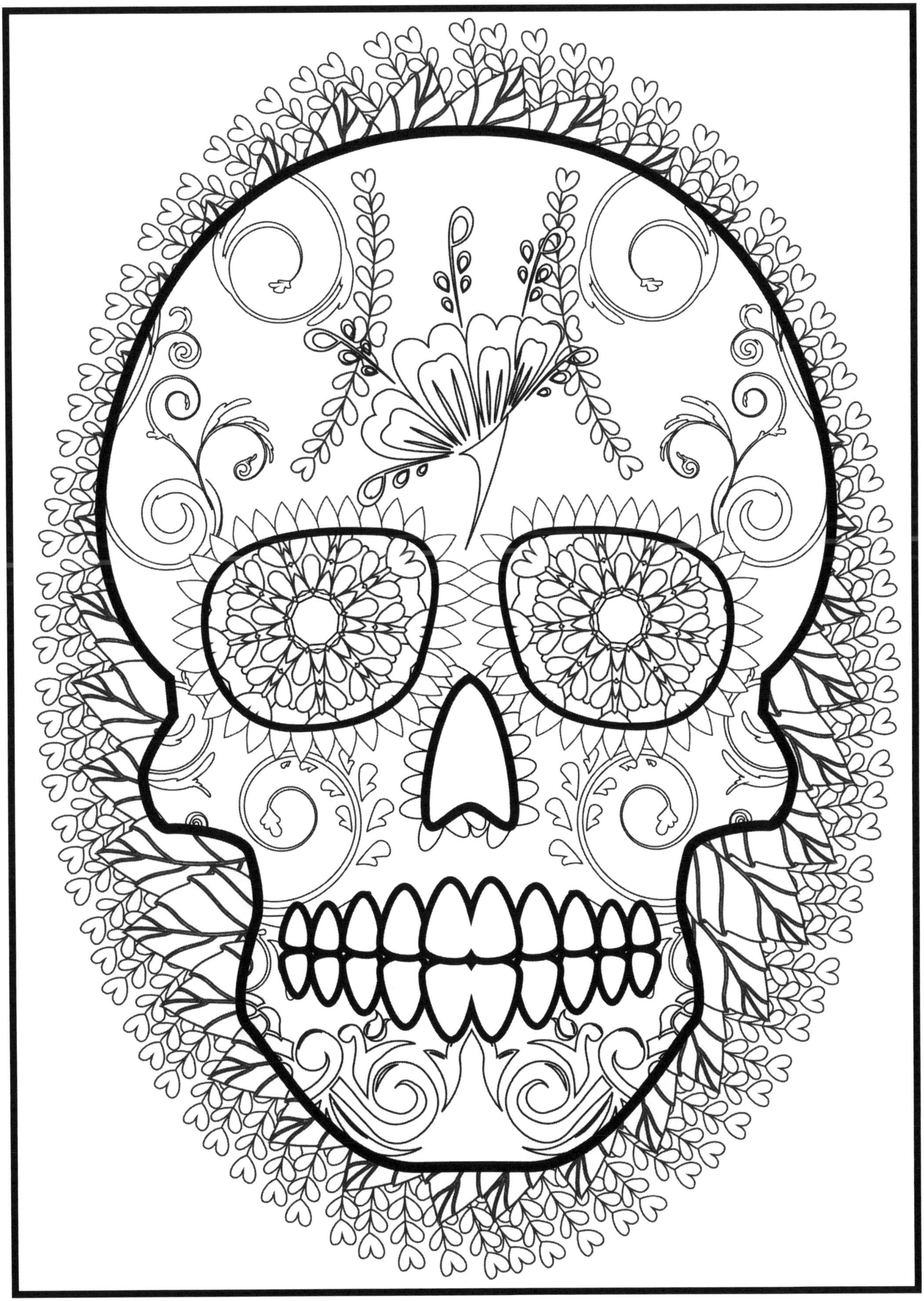

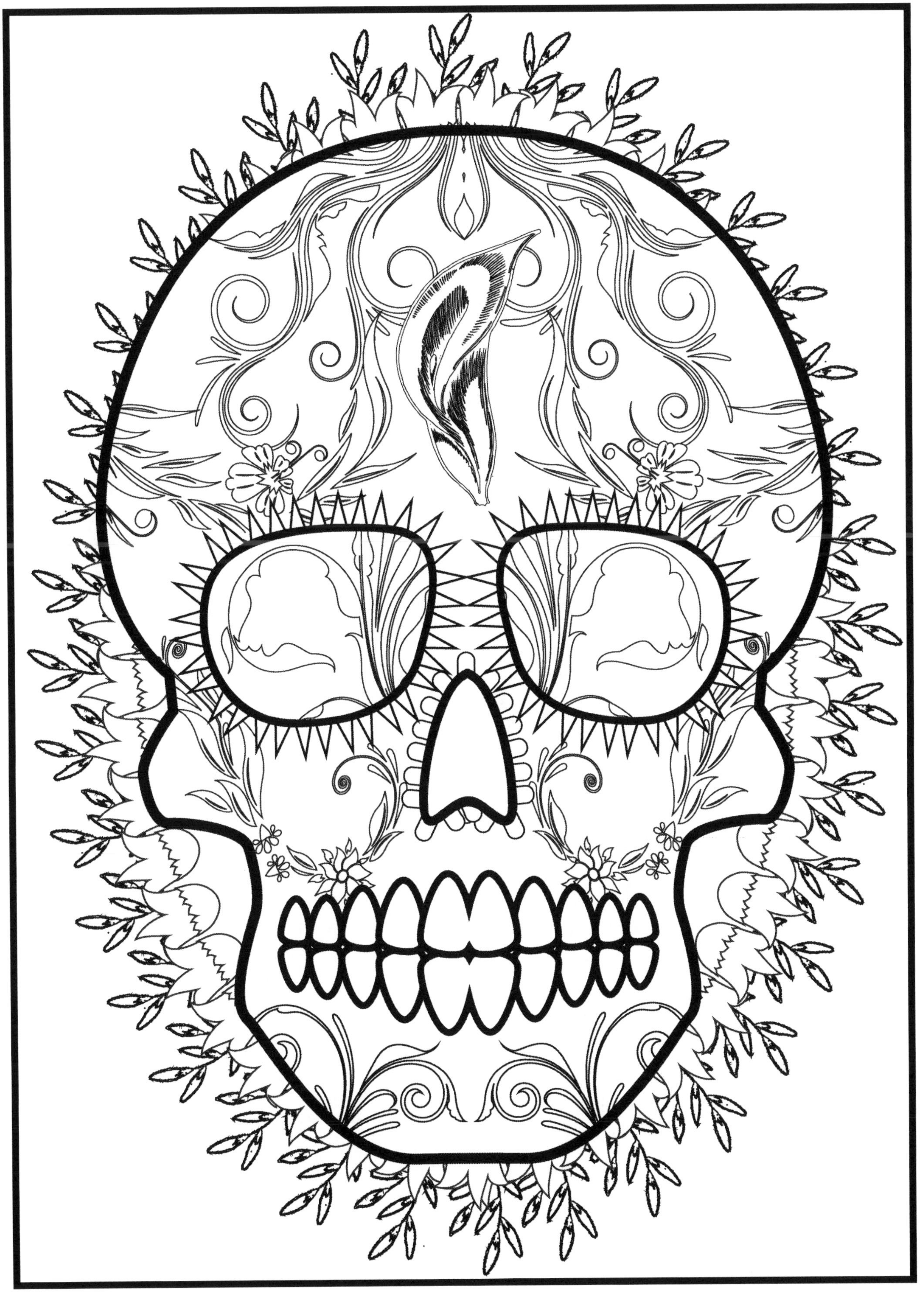

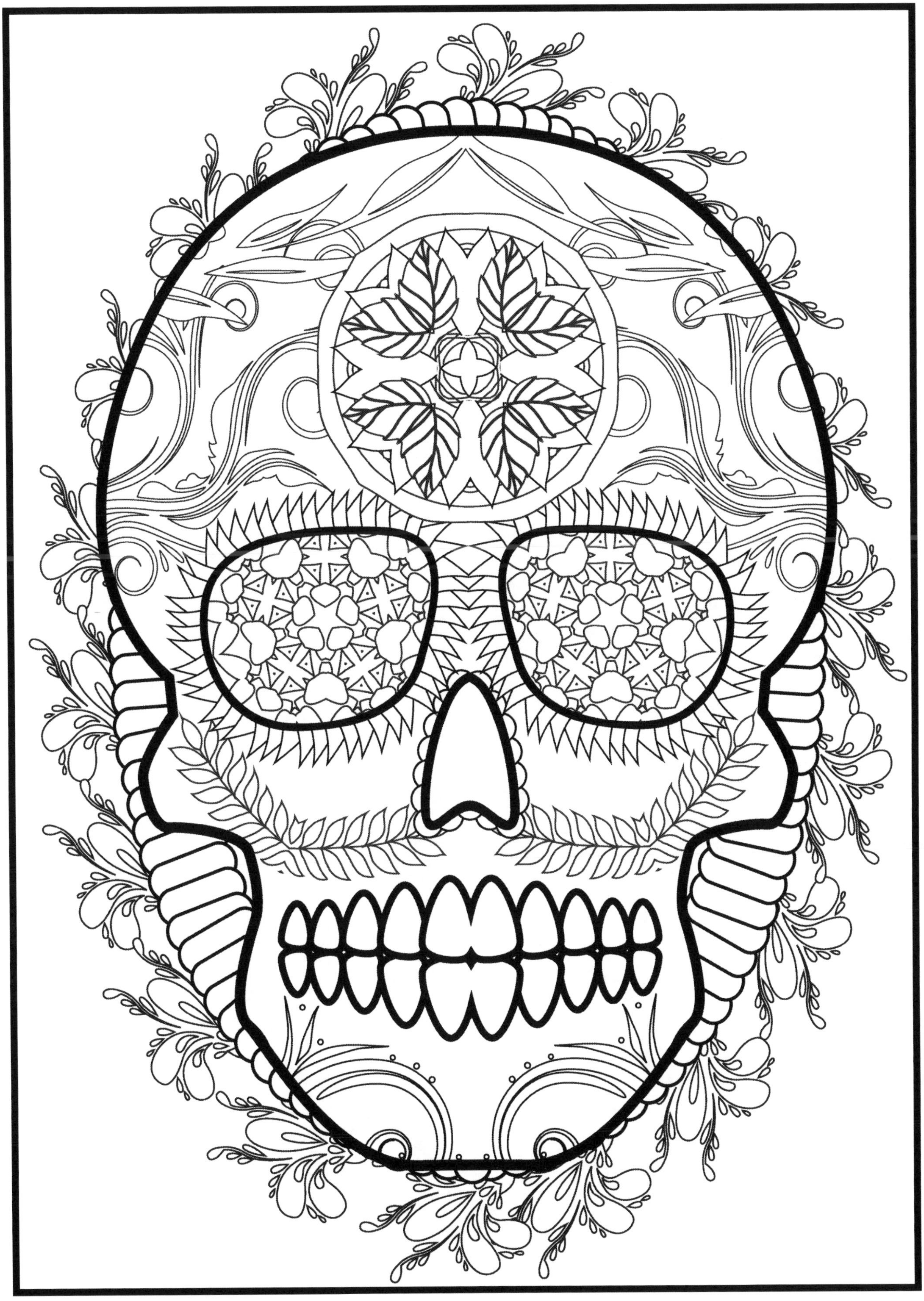

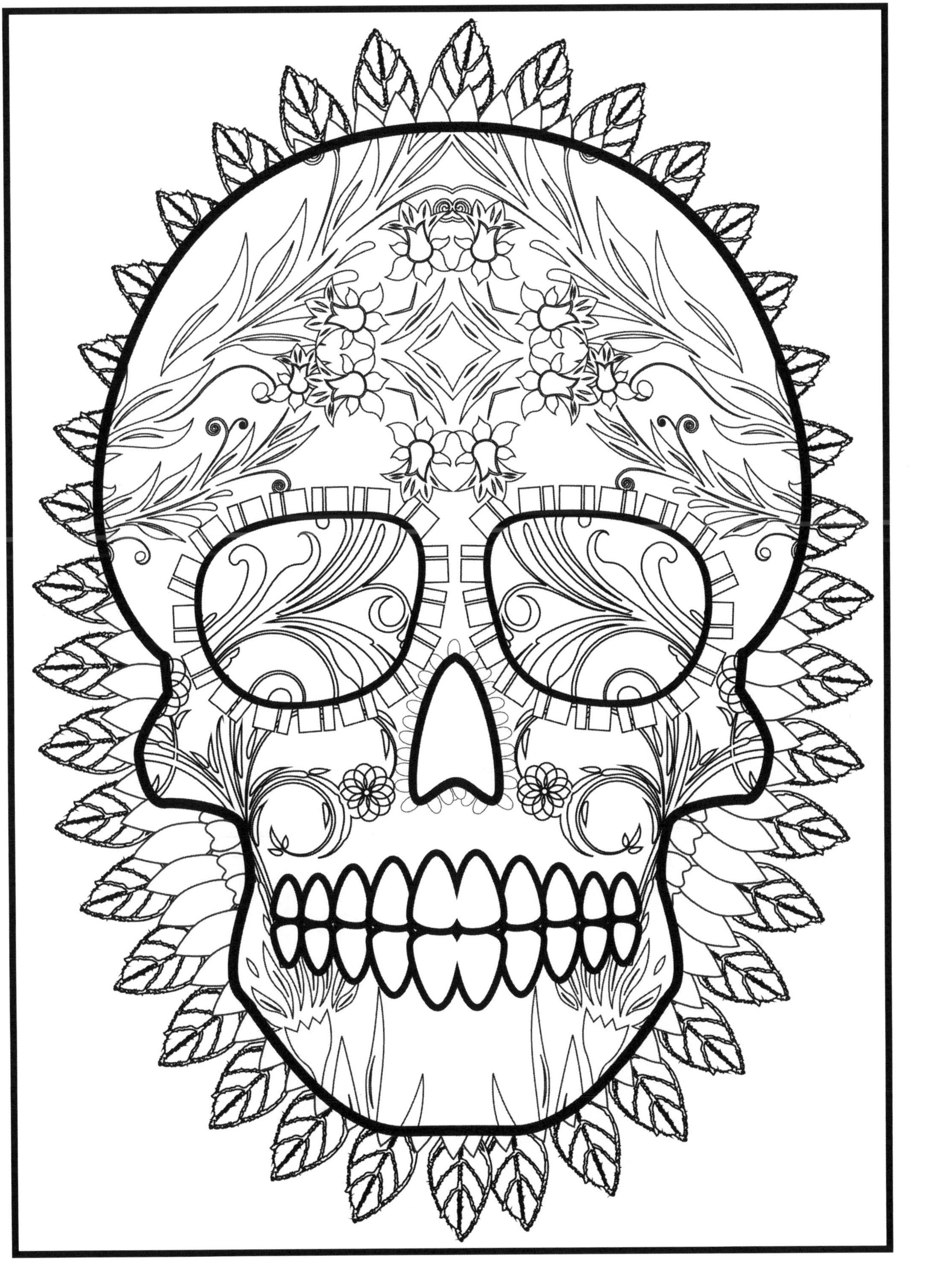

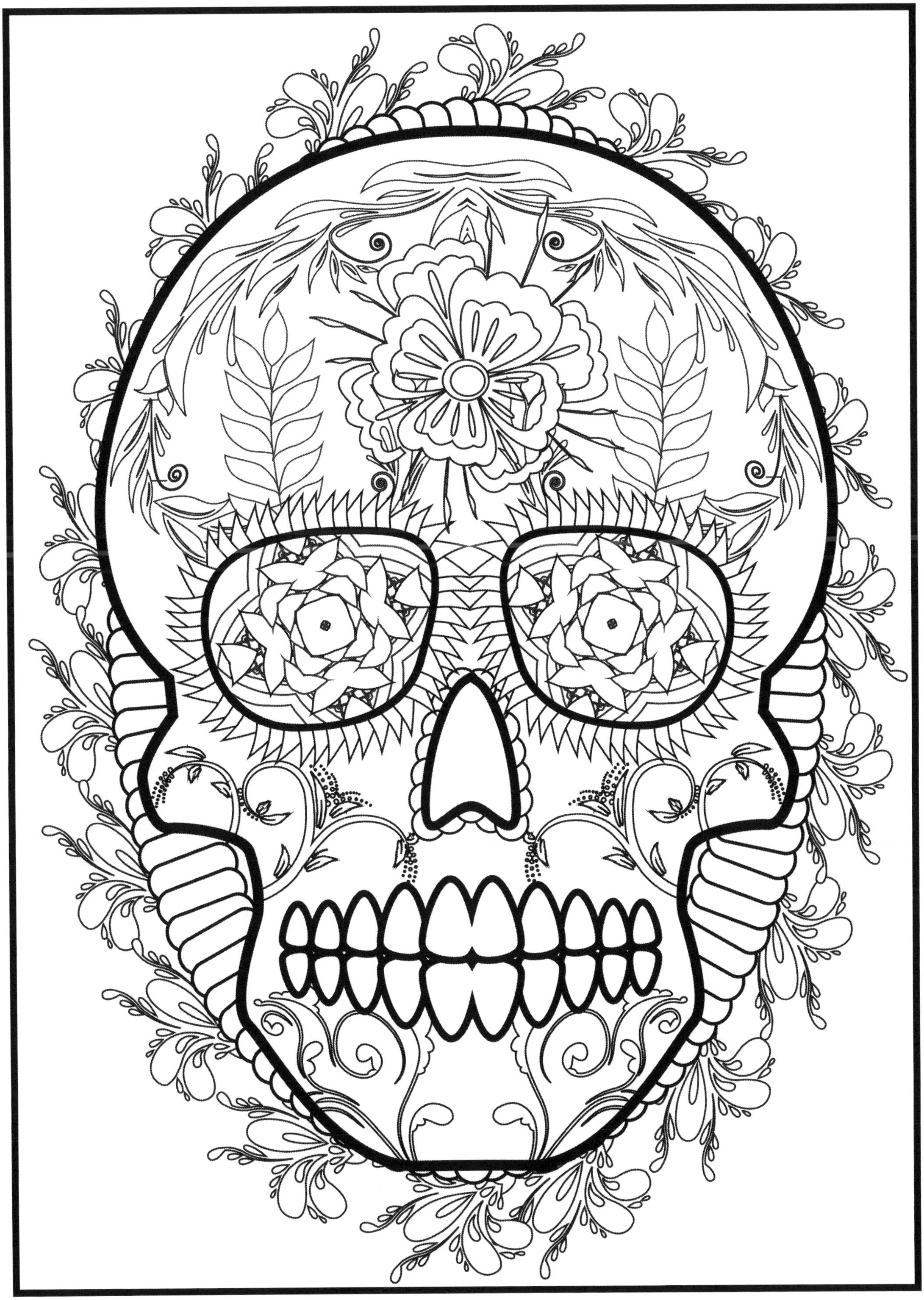

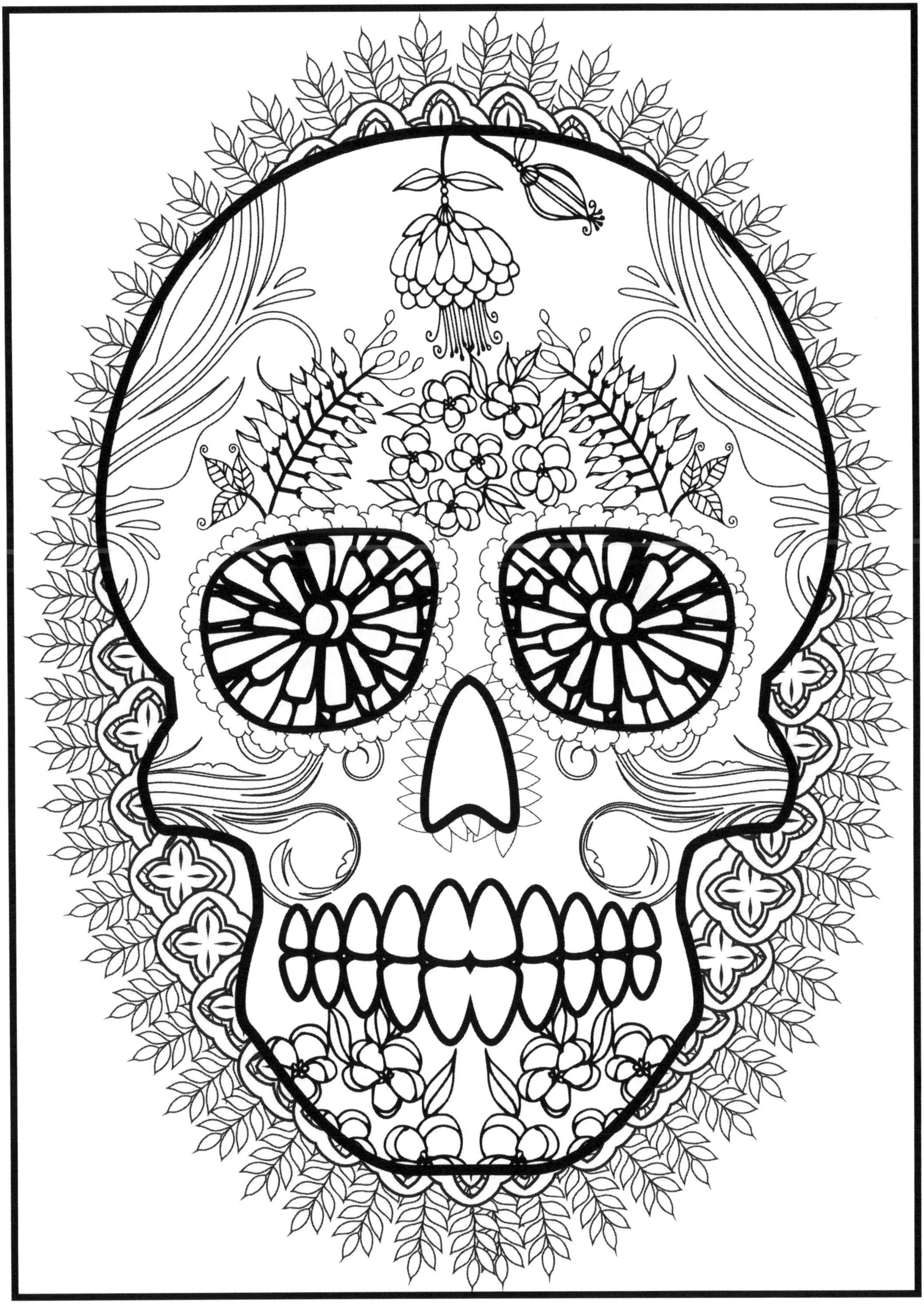

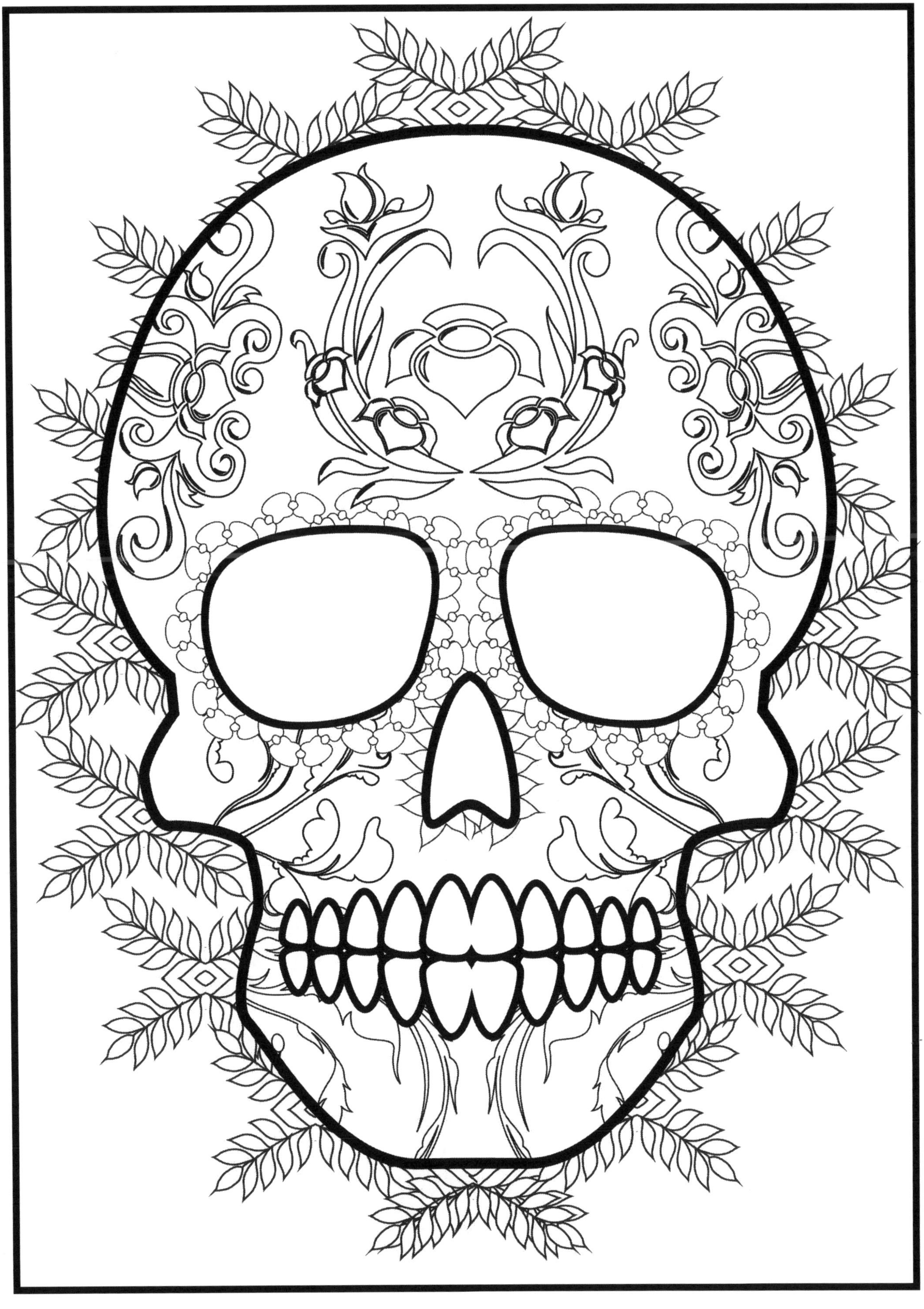

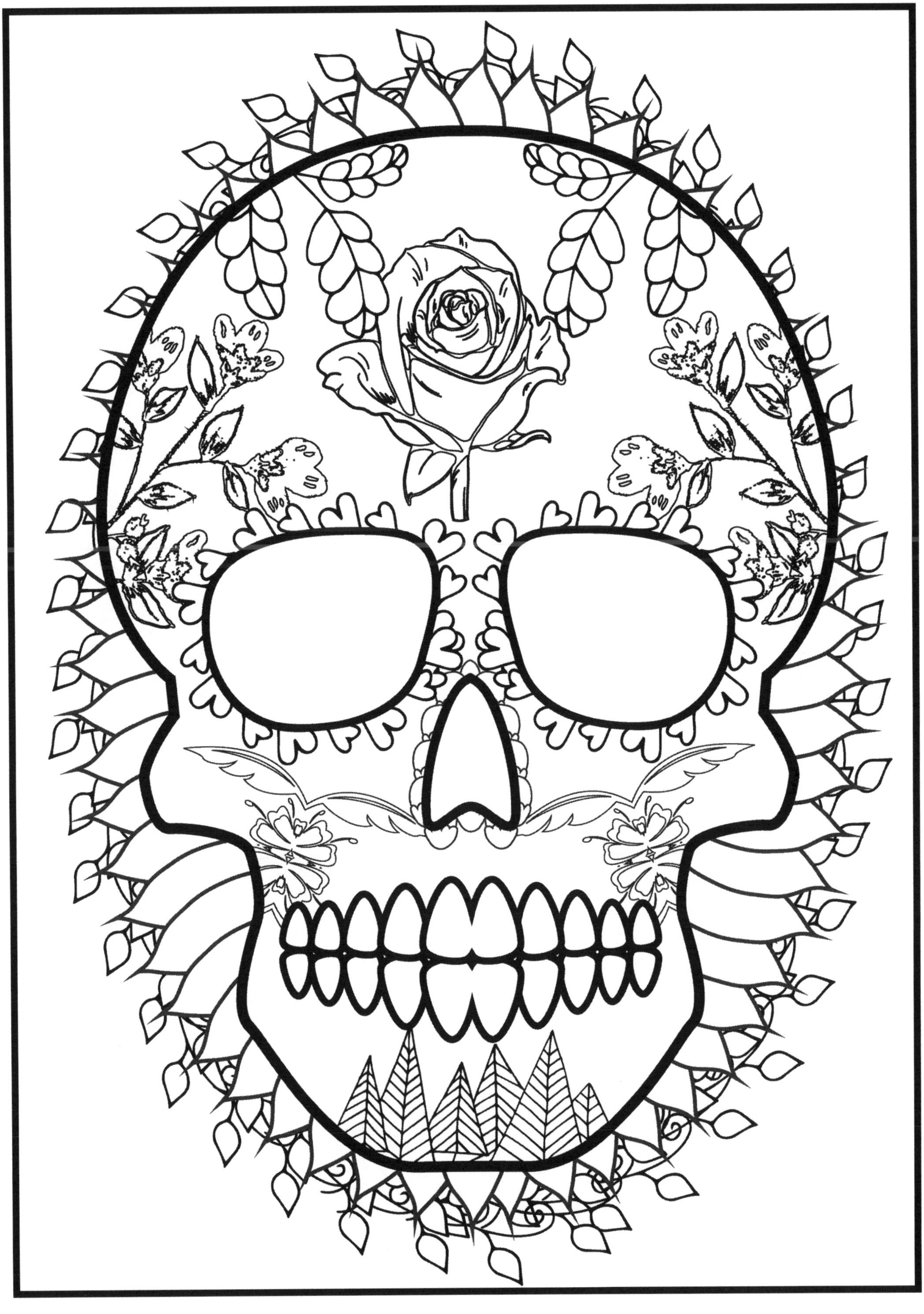

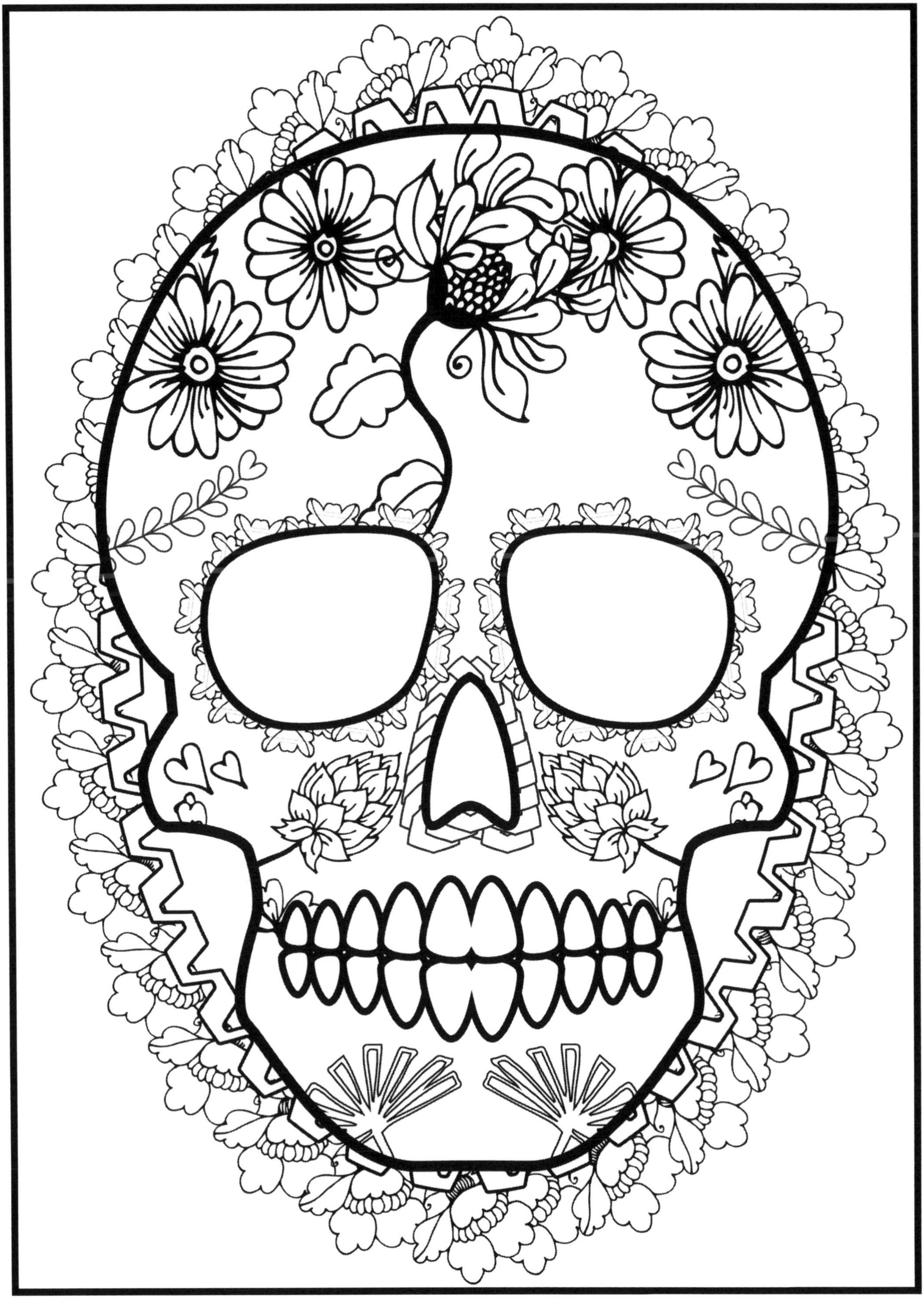

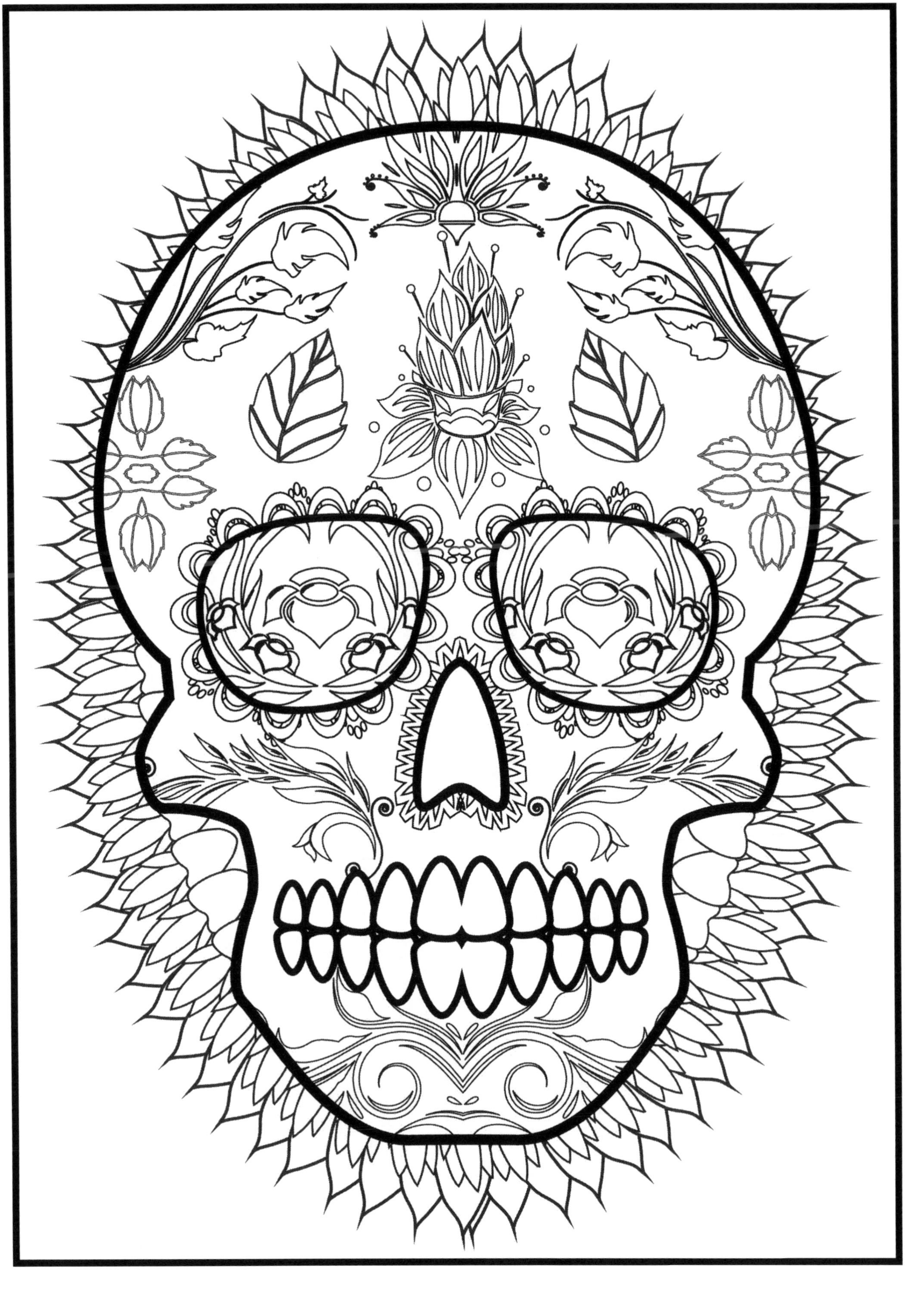

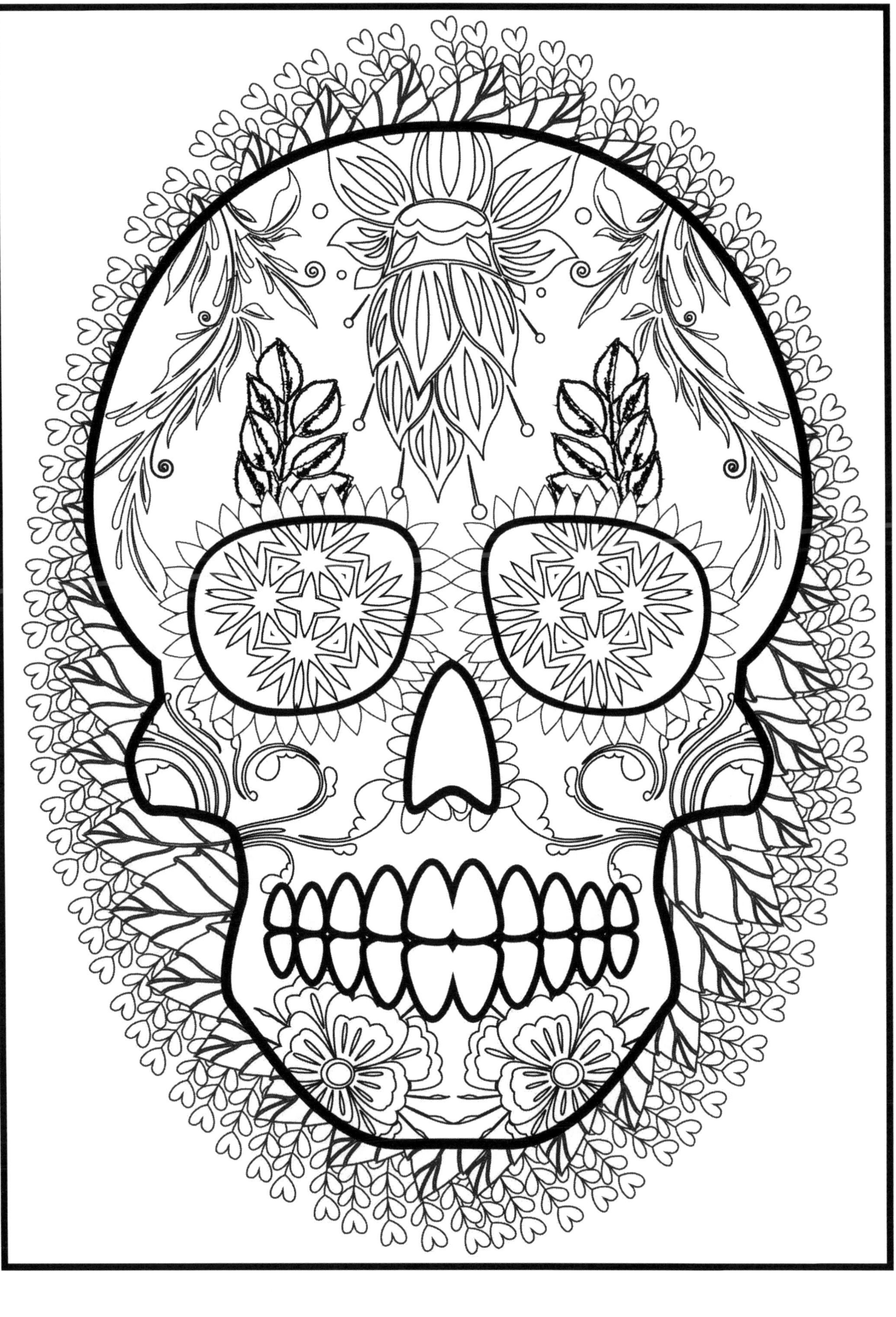

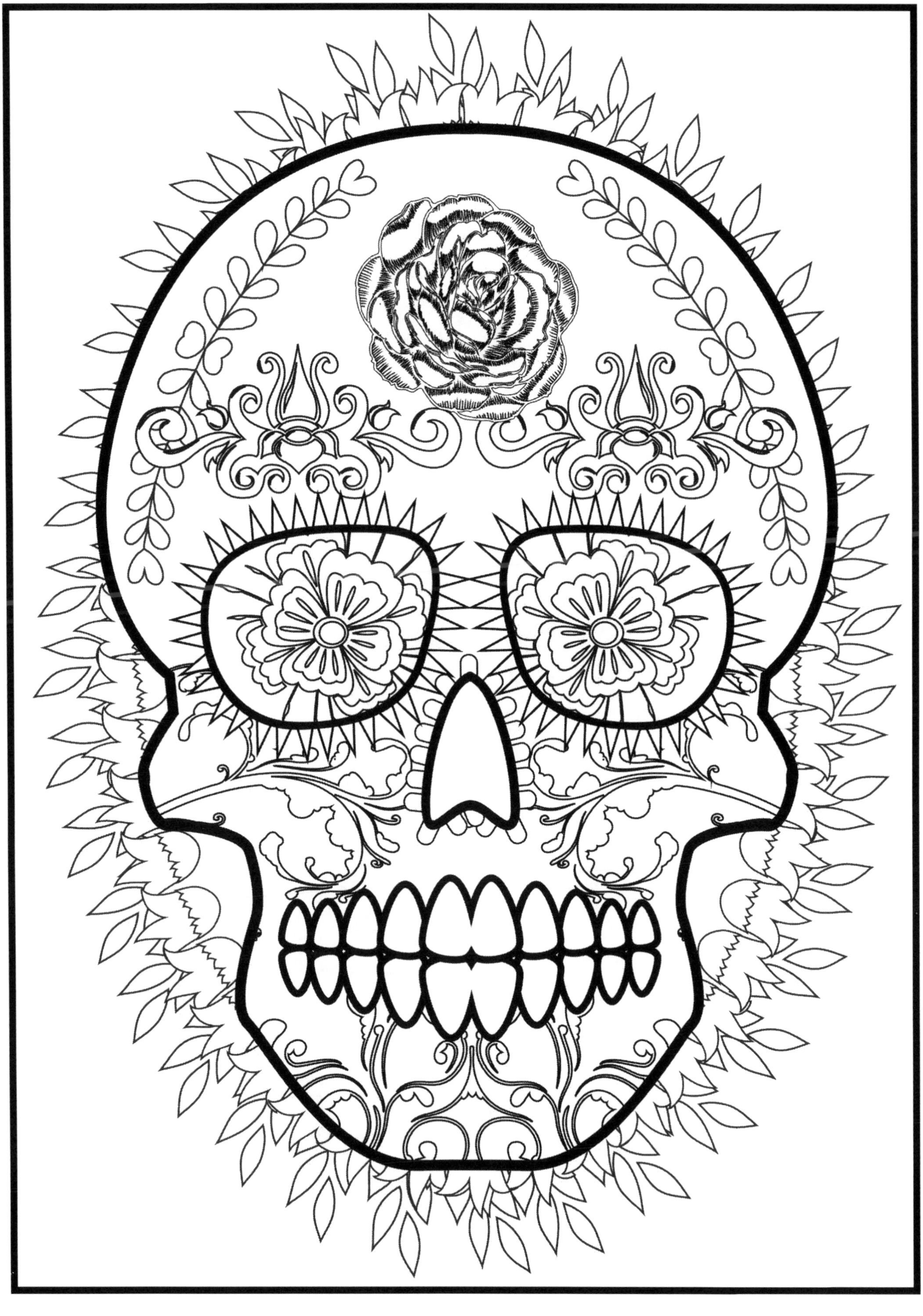

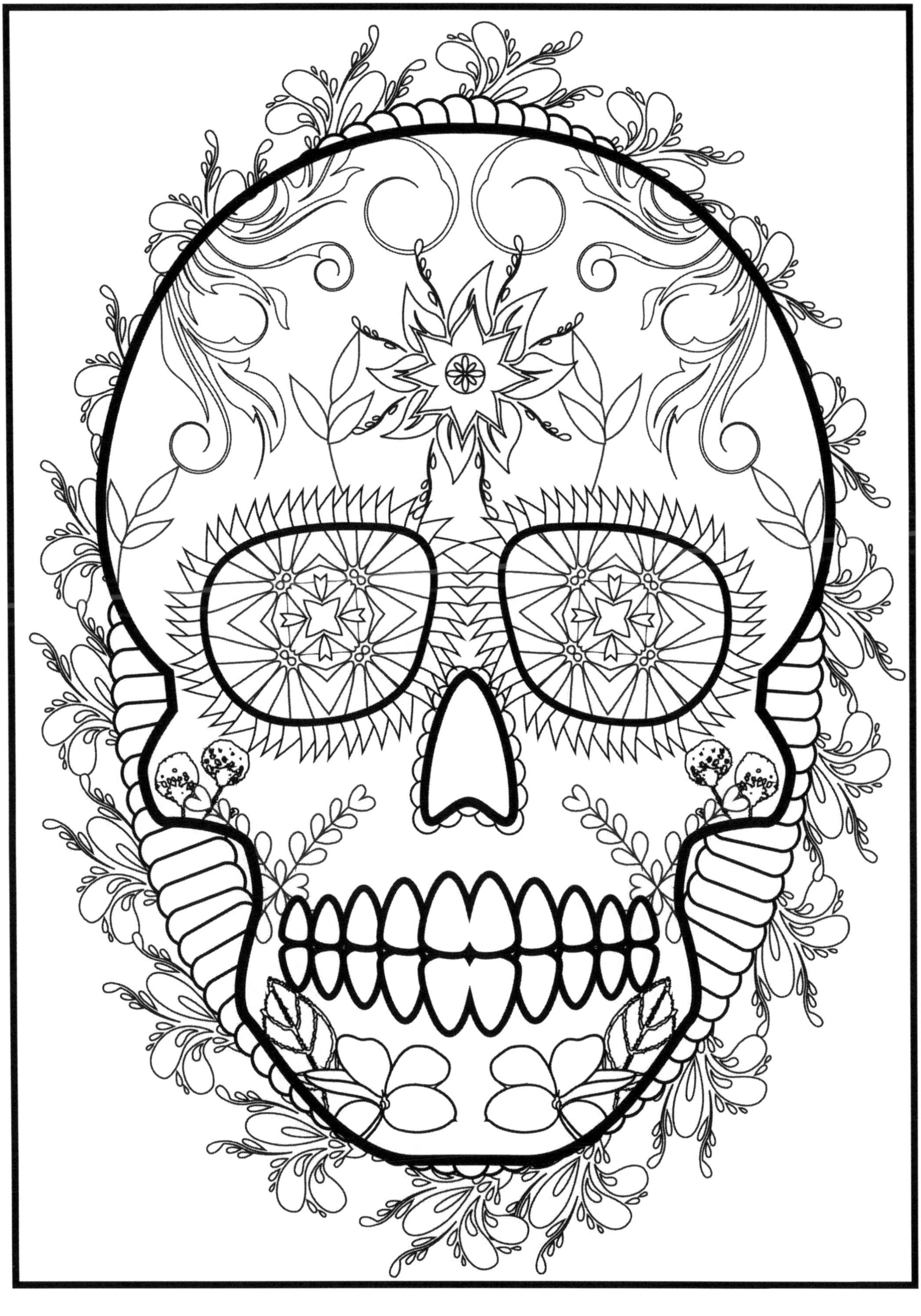

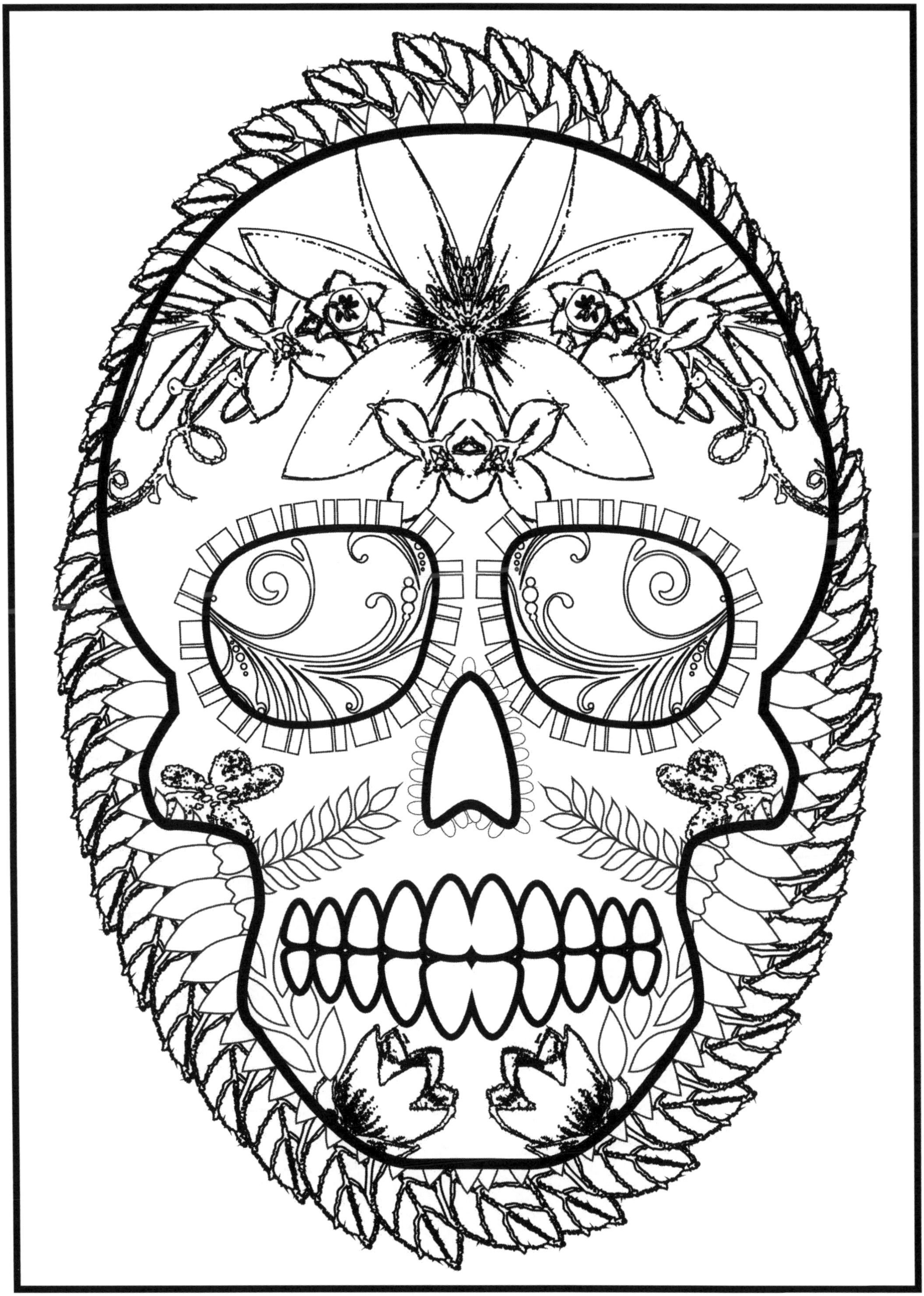

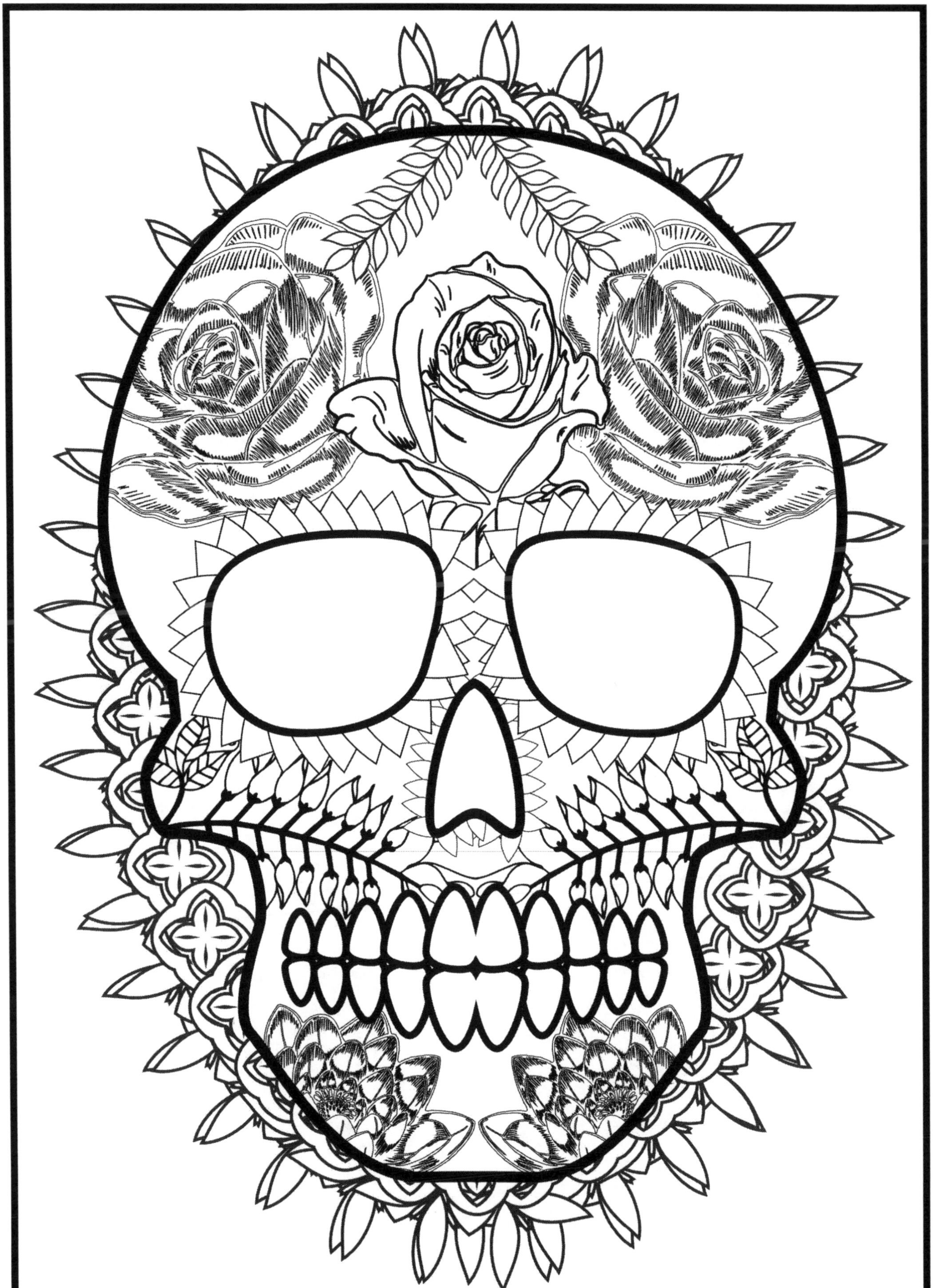

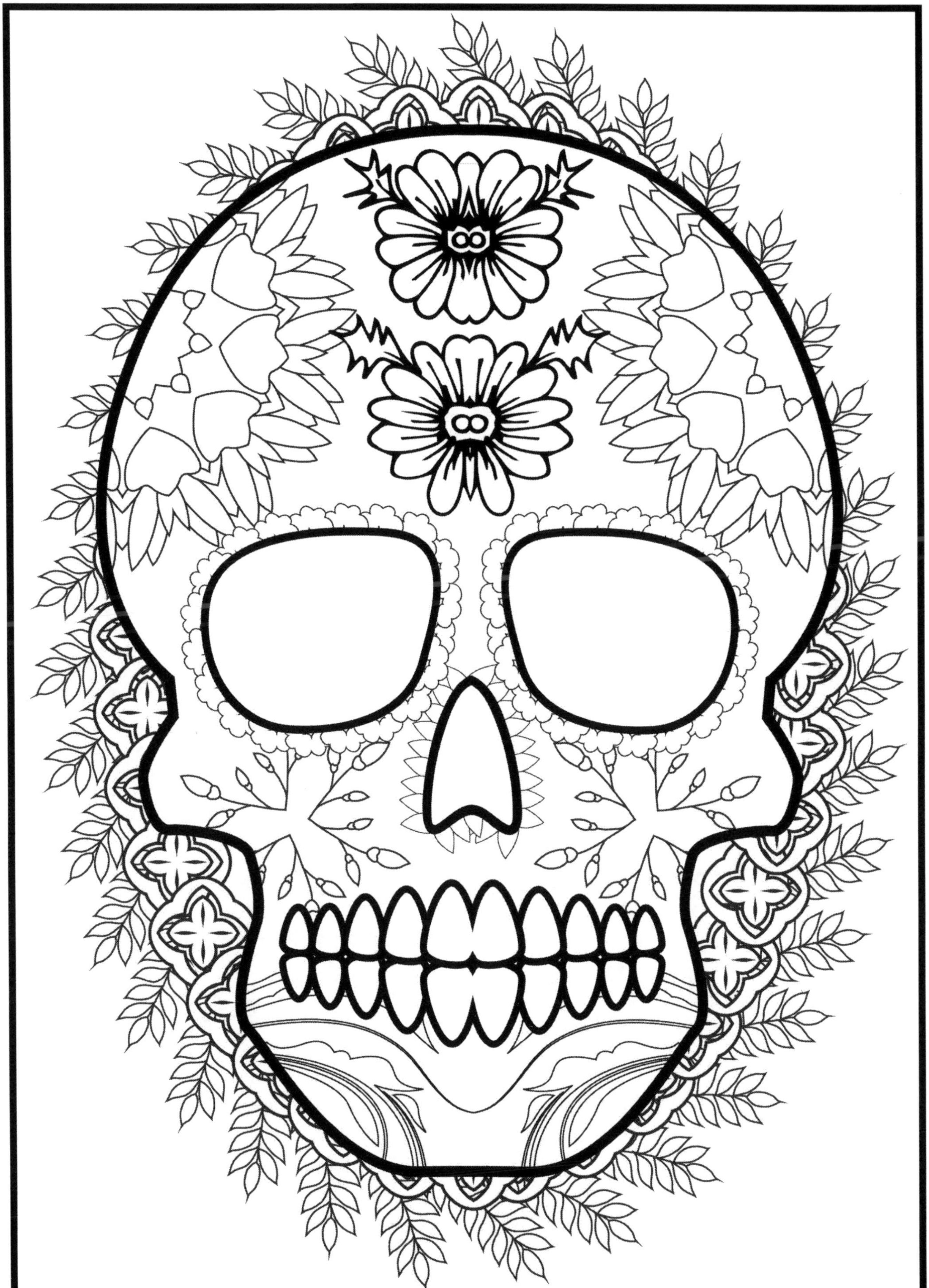

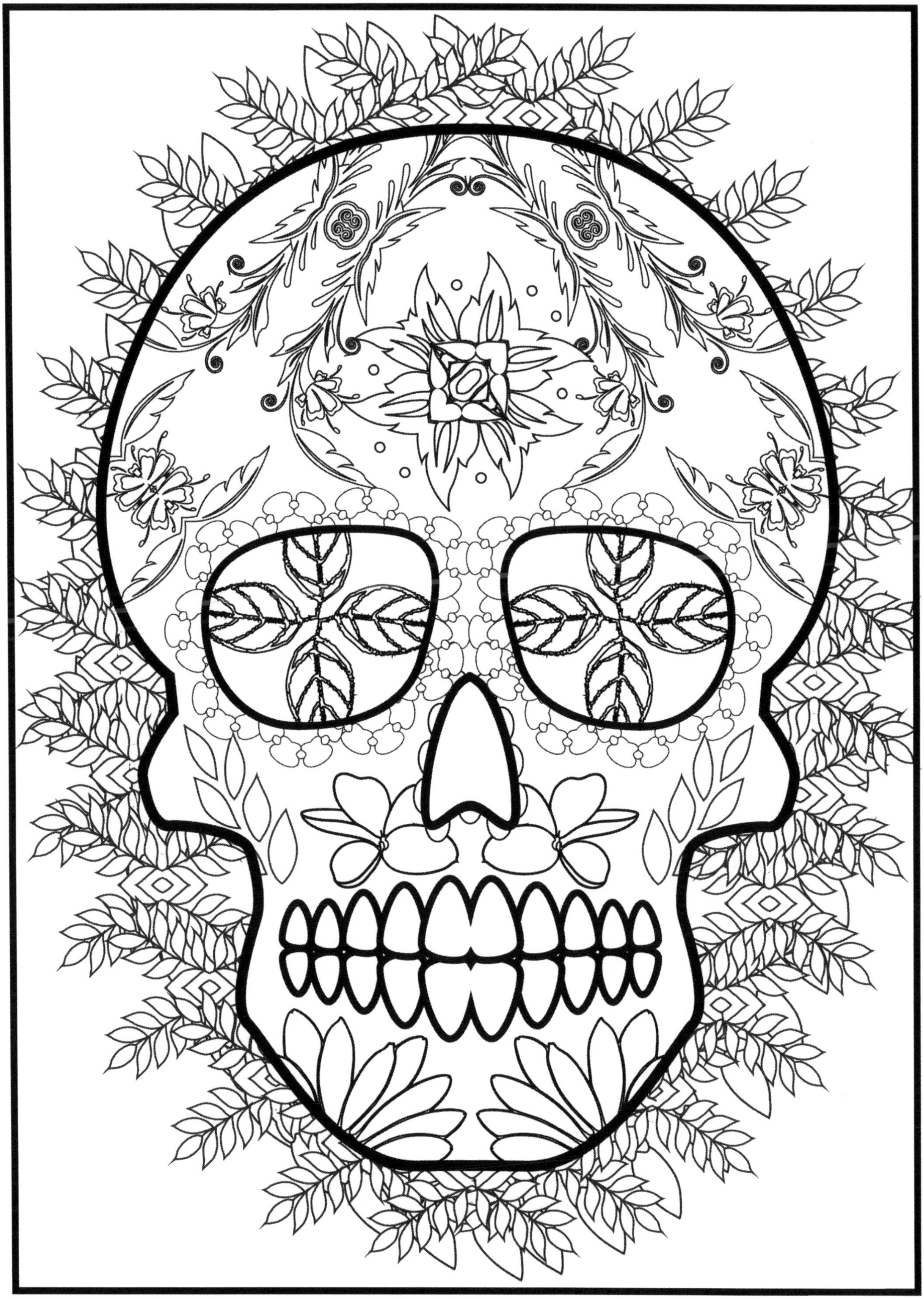

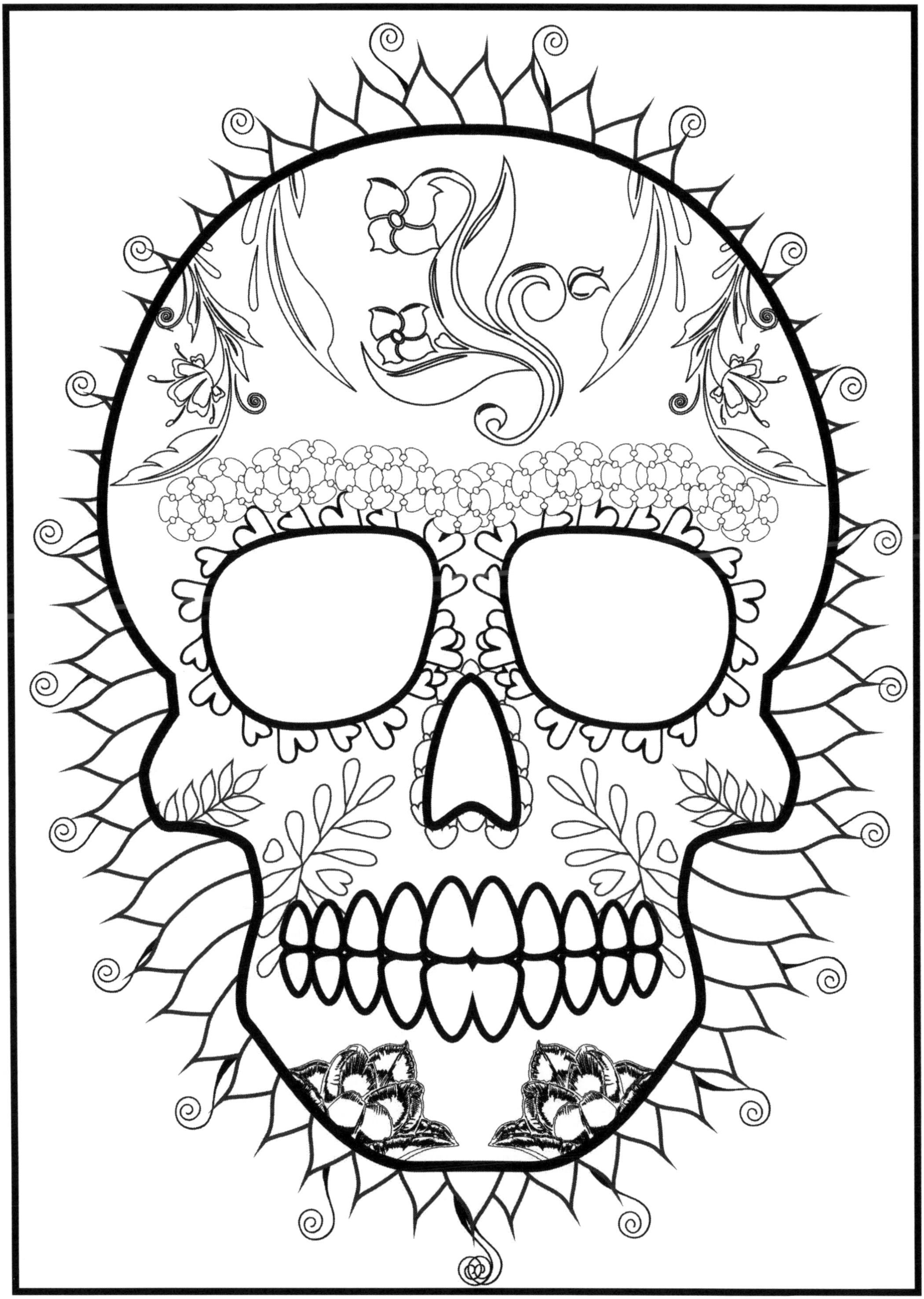

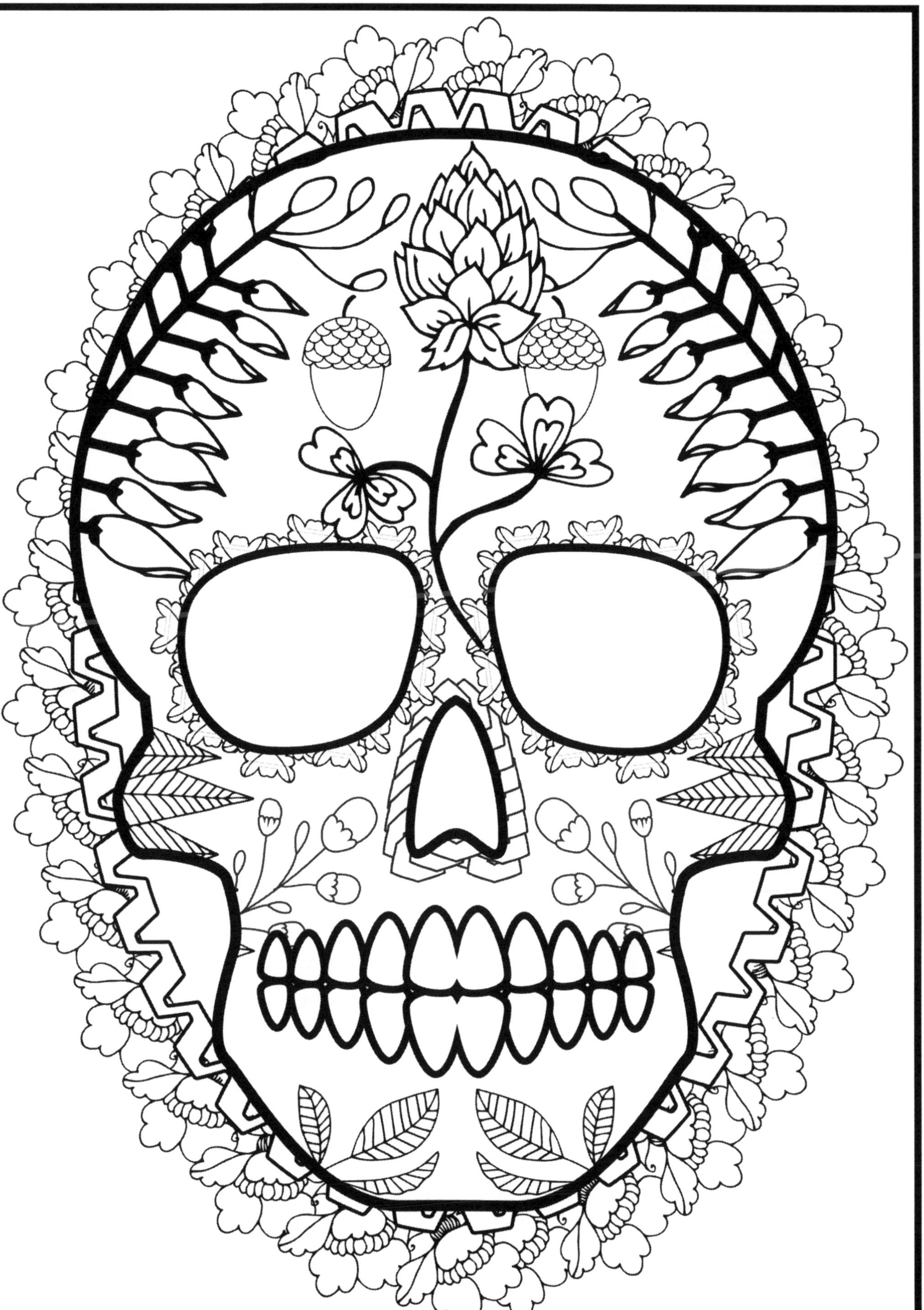

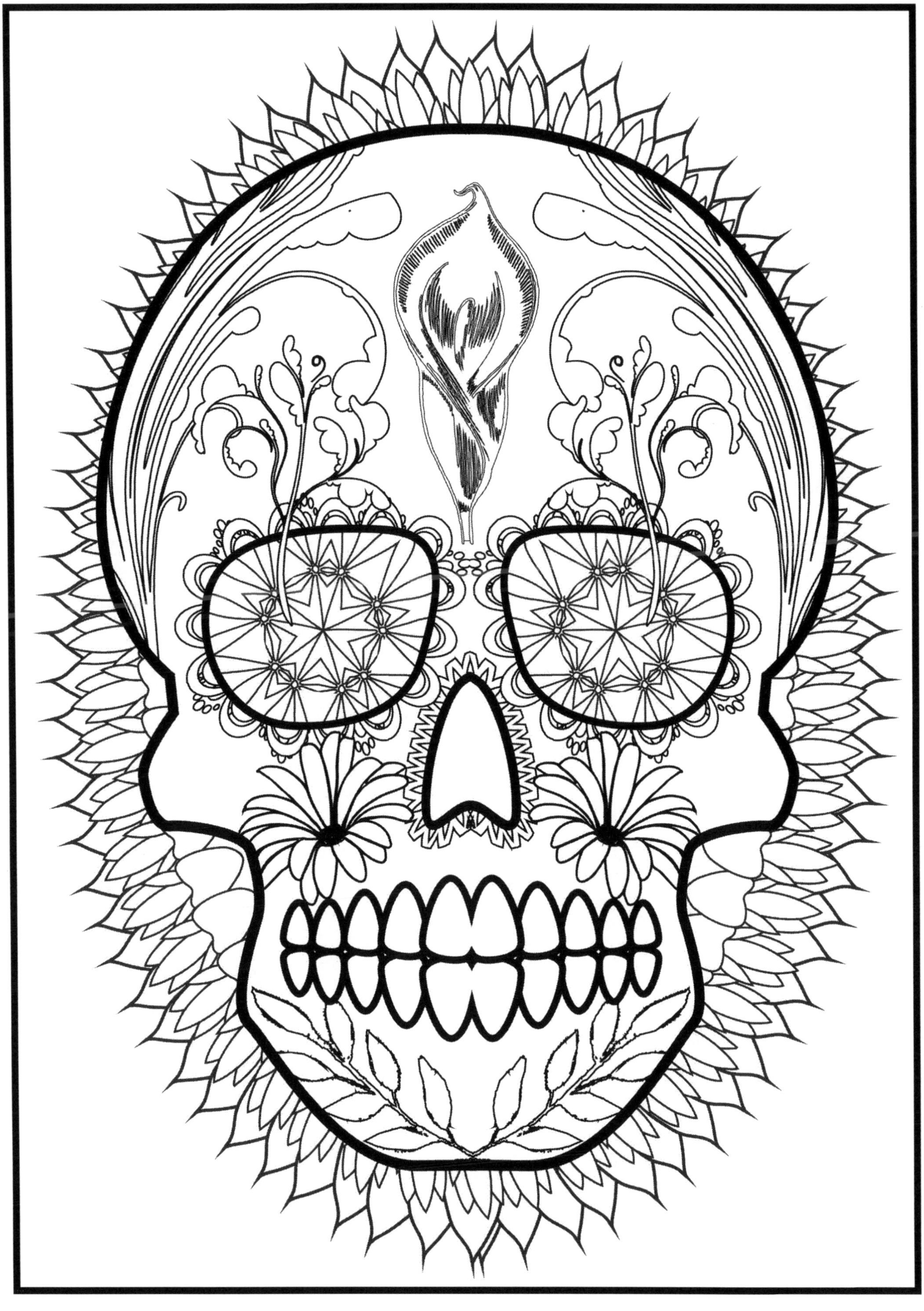

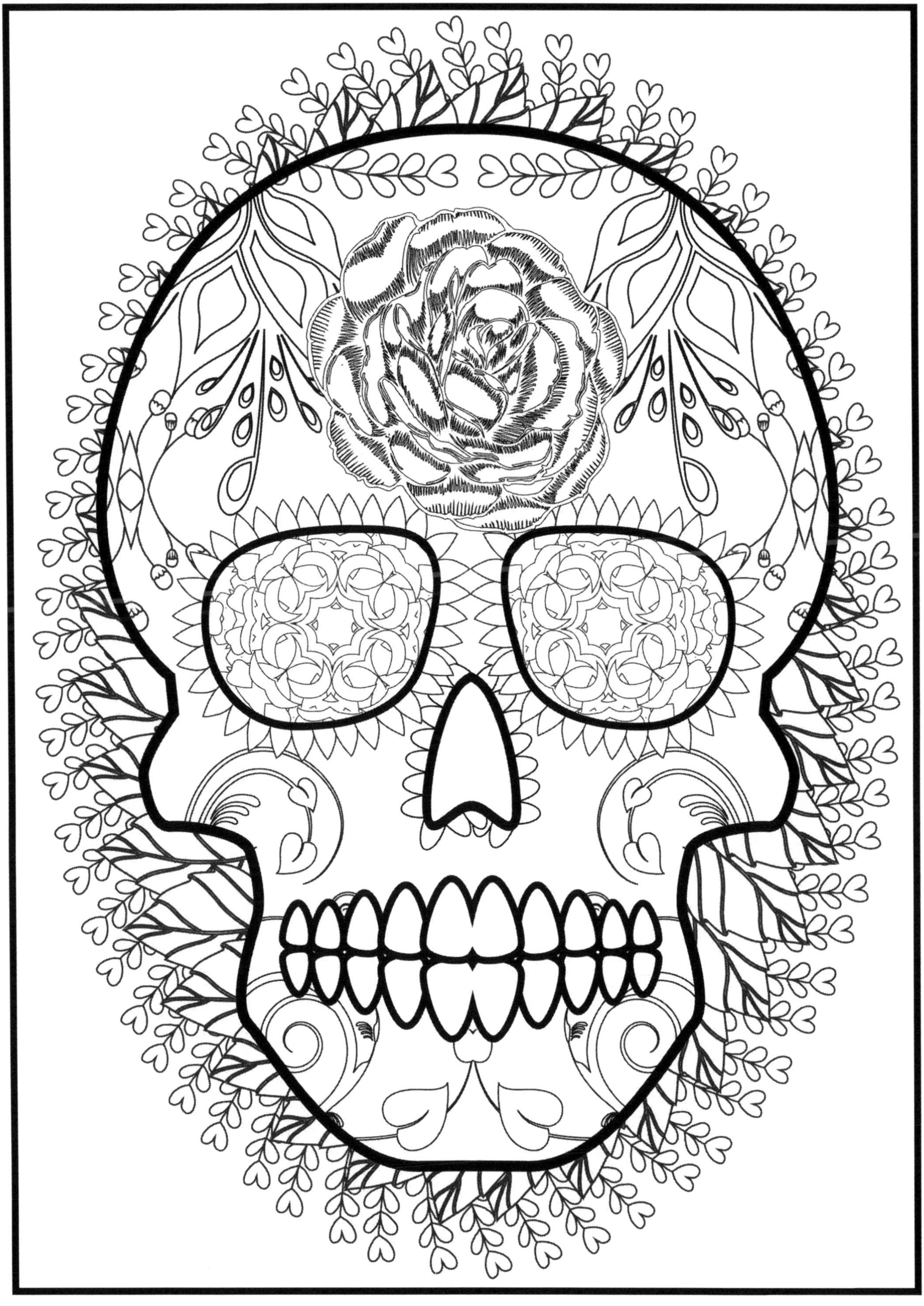

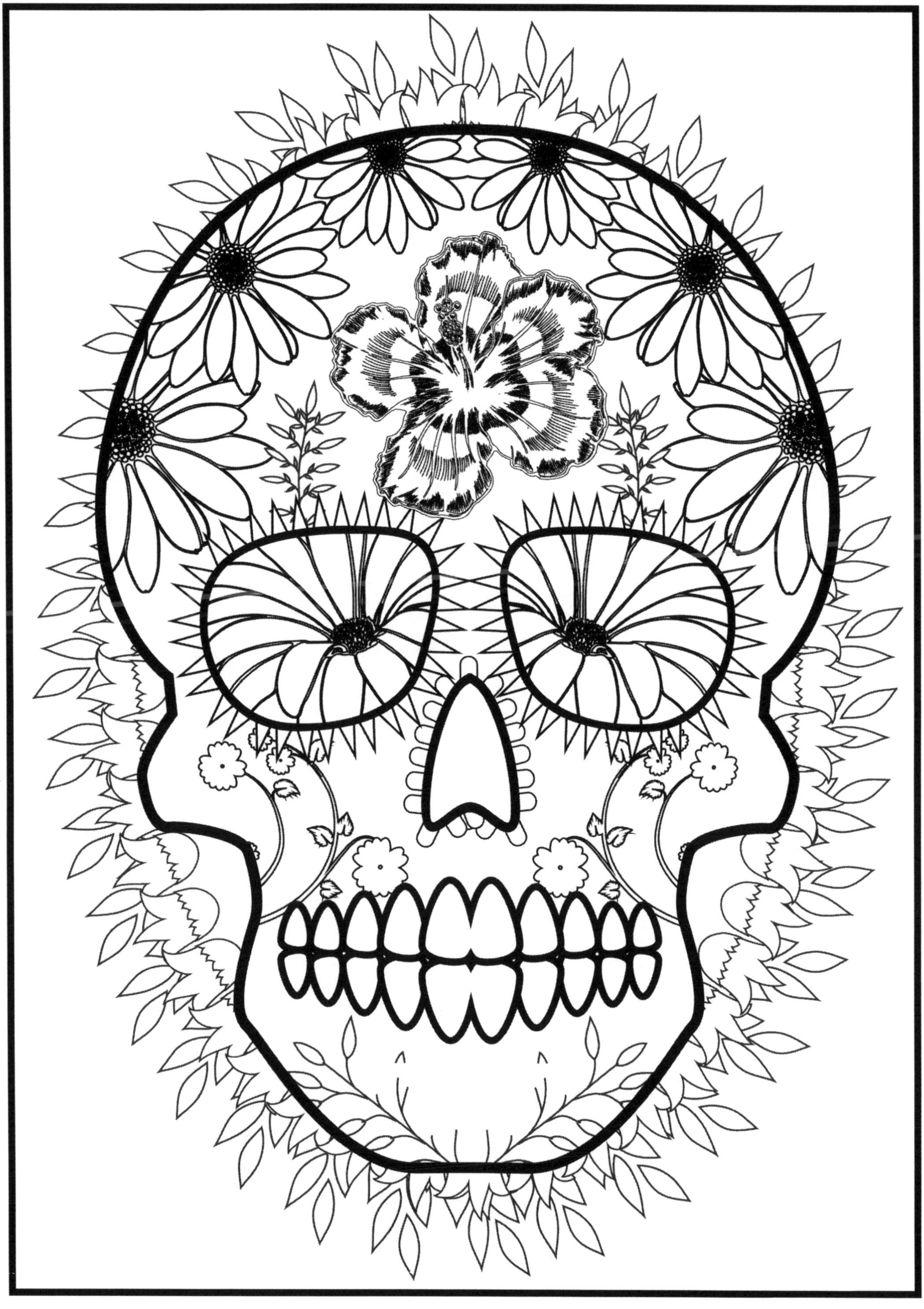

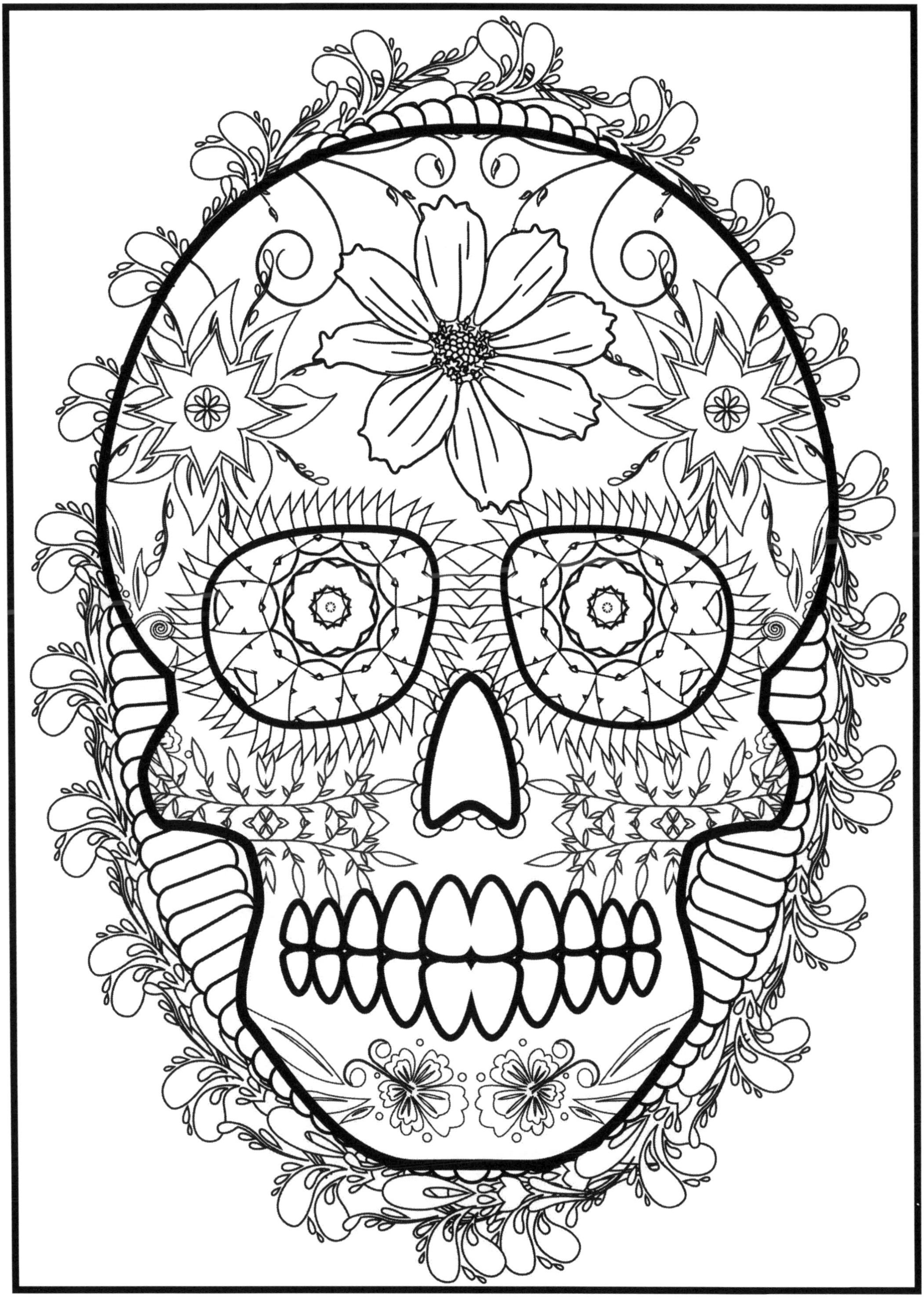

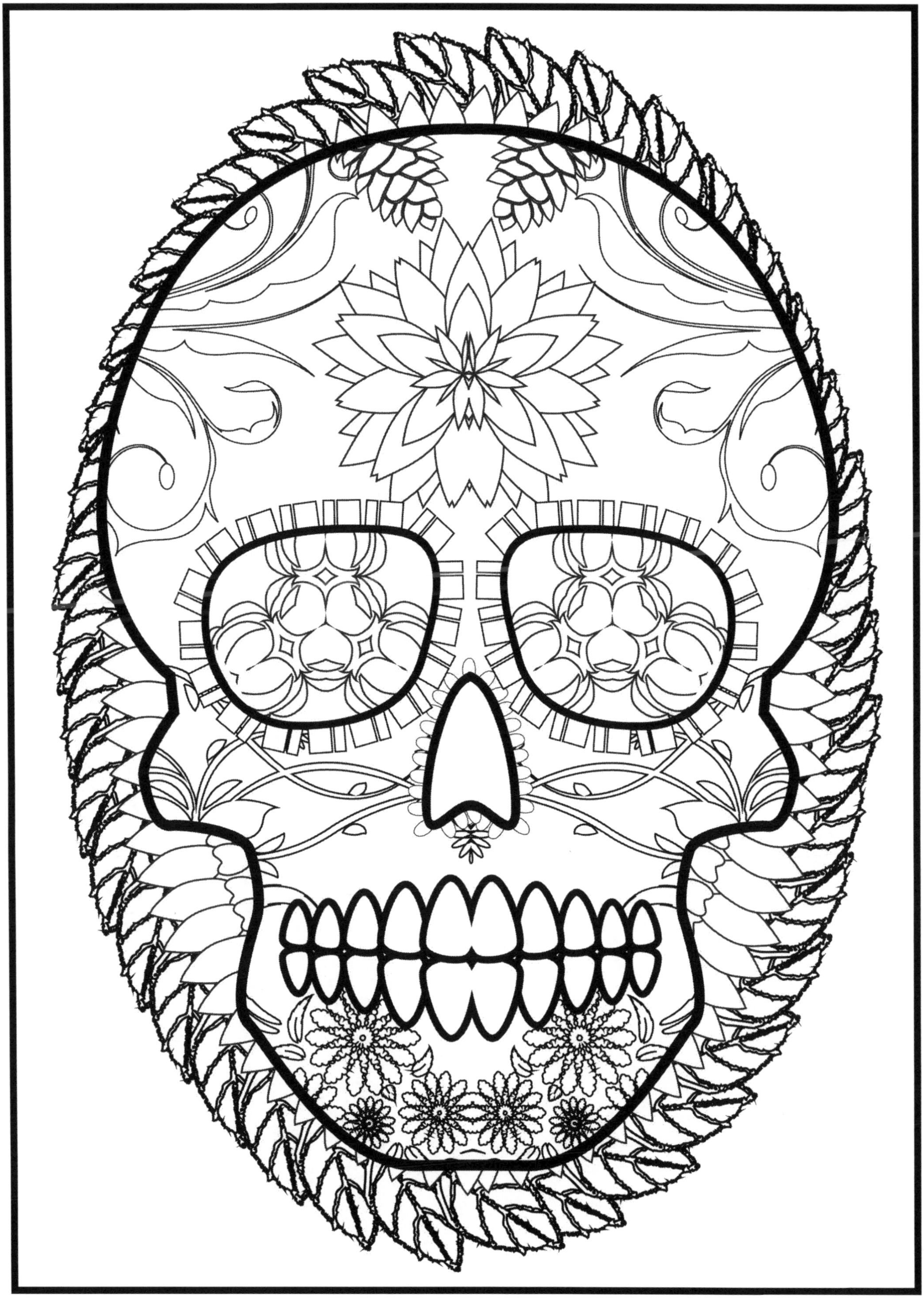

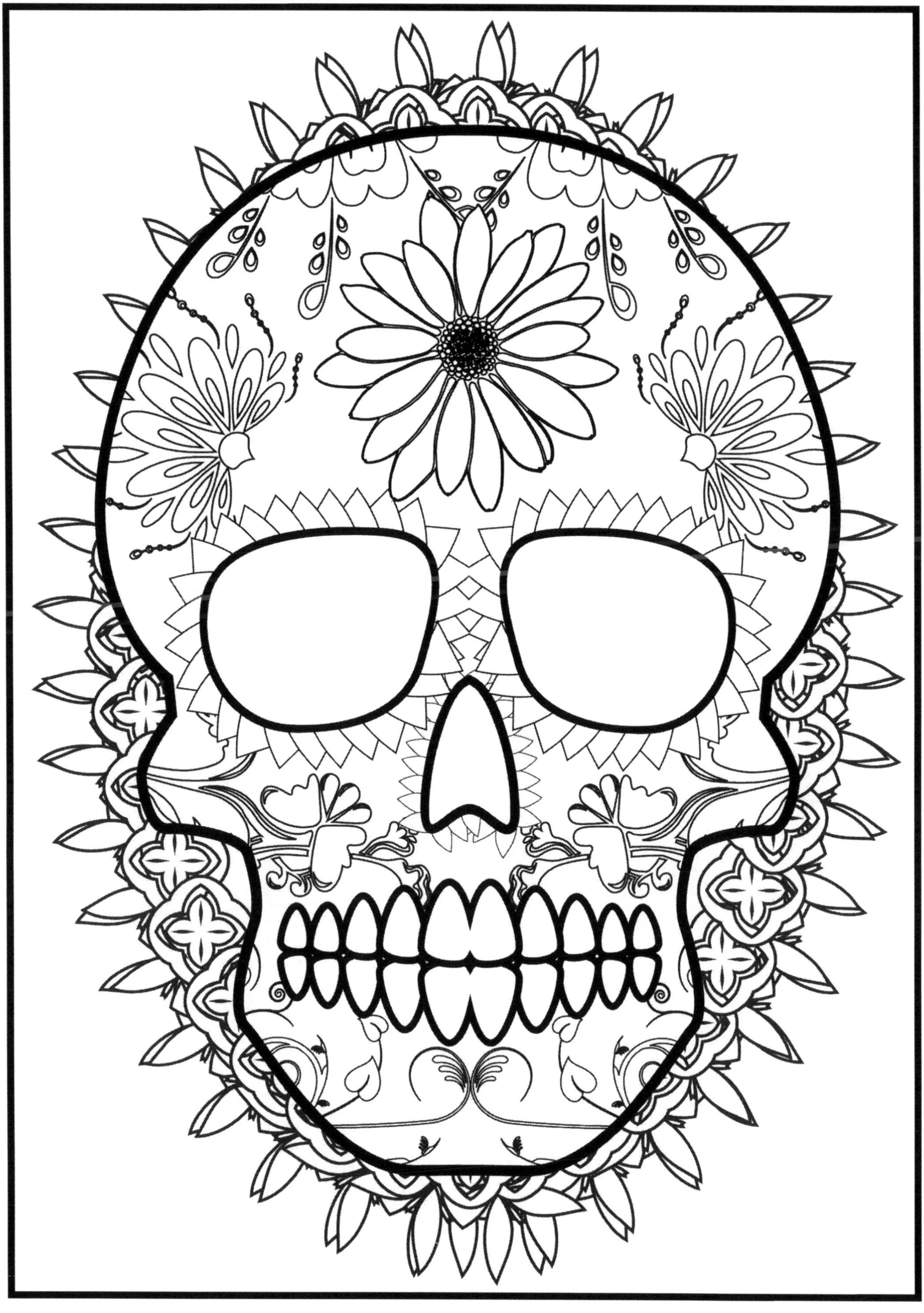

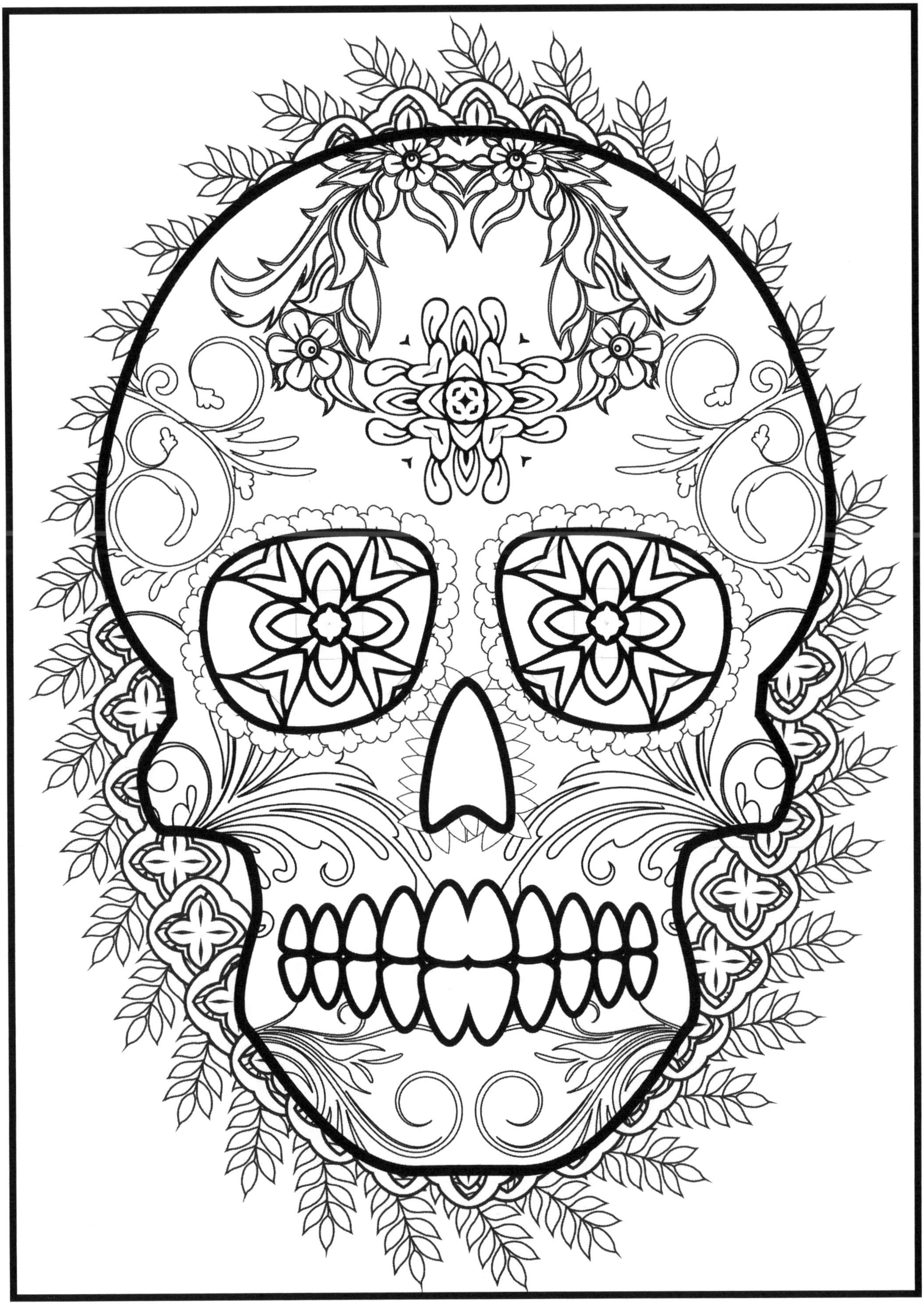

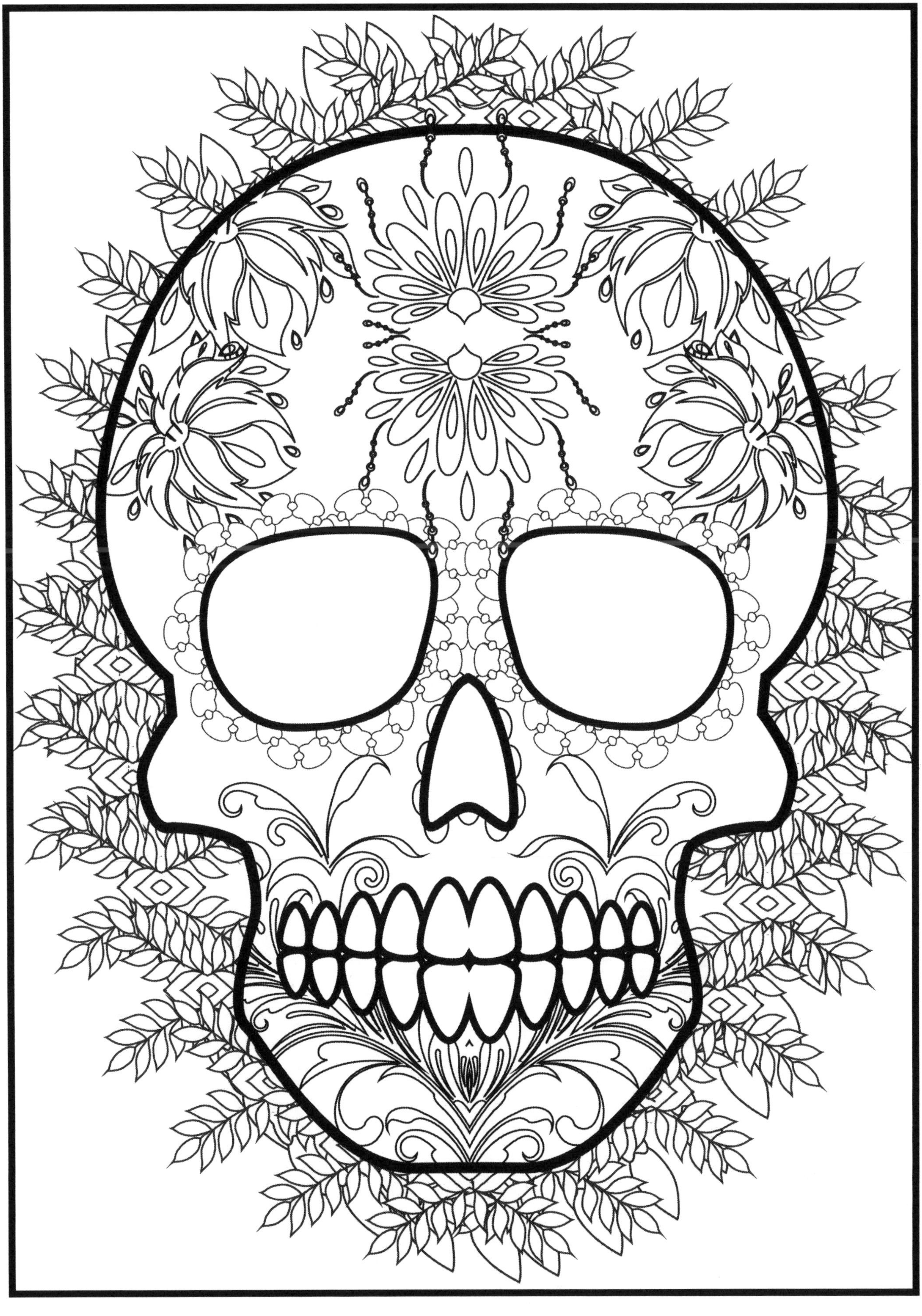

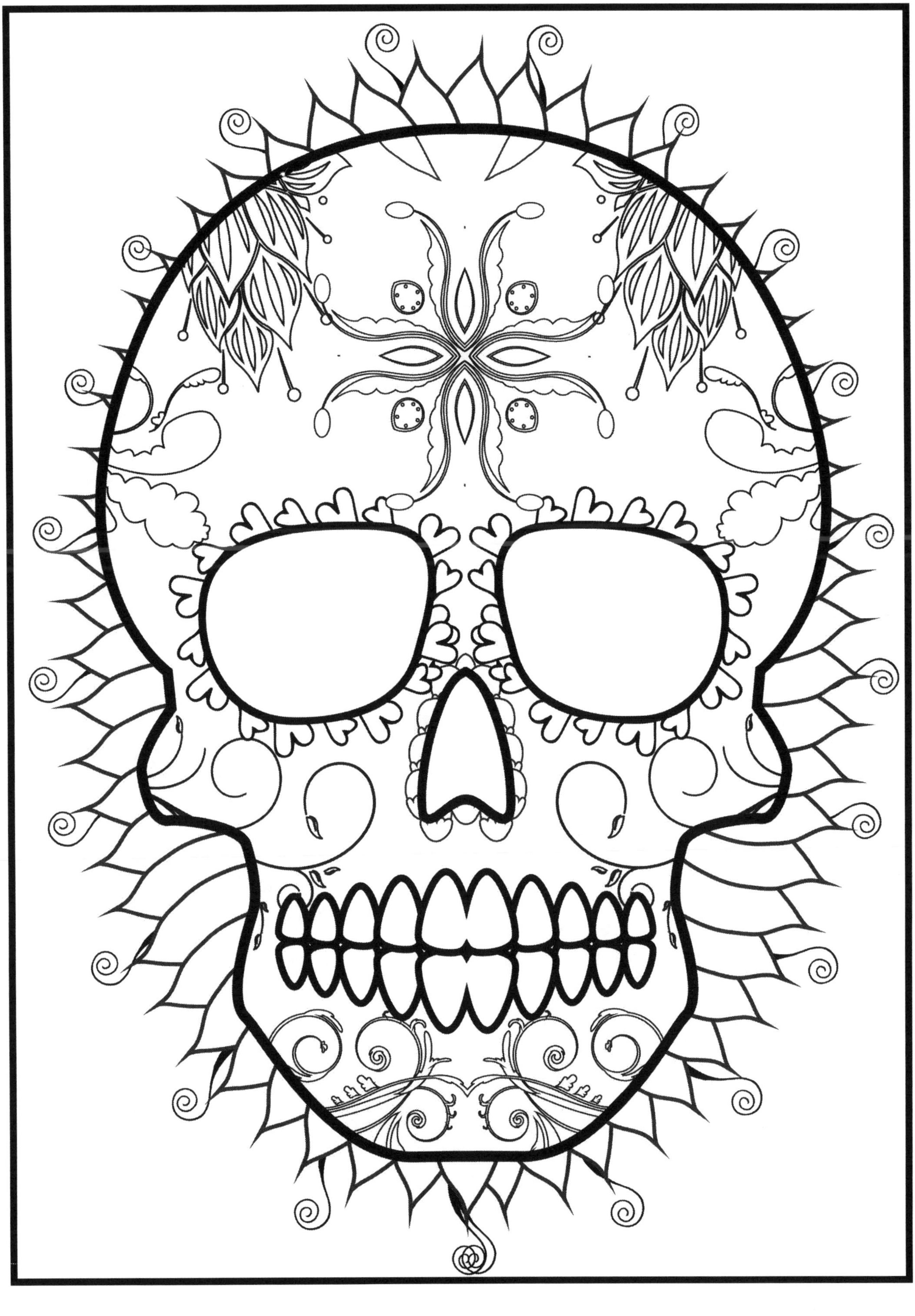

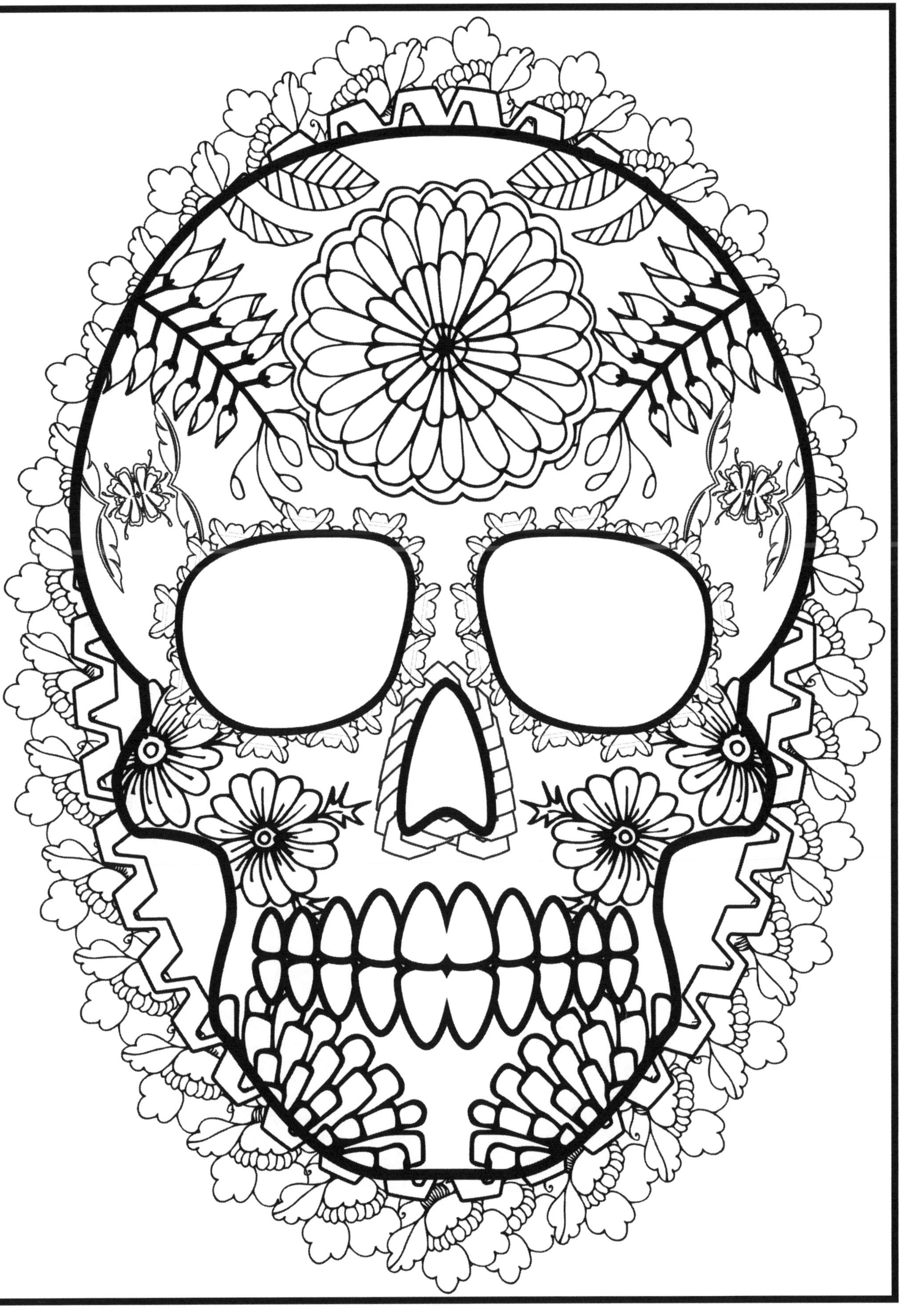

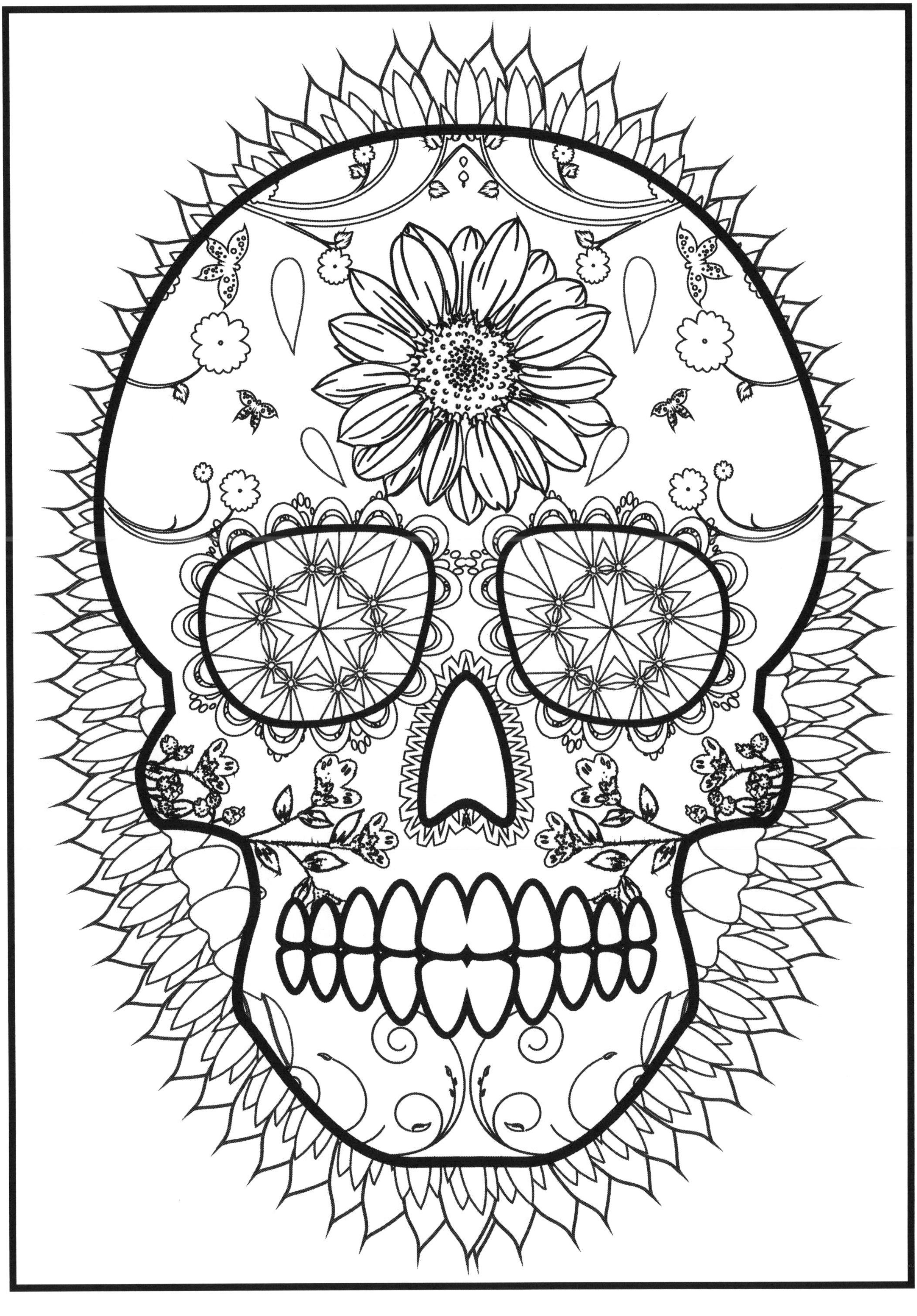